The Fairytale Doll Book

VALERIE JANITCH

Introduced by
THE THREE BEARS

A David & Charles Craft Book

ACKNOWLEDGEMENTS

My very special thanks to Melvin Grey, whose magical photography made all my fairytales come true.

My thanks also to Josiah Wedgwood & Son Ltd, for all the china which appears in the photographs. The Three Bears and the Mad Hatter are most grateful to Catherine Hart for helping them to choose it.

I would like to thank Julie Darby, editor of *Popular Crafts* magazine, for allowing me to reproduce the Sugar Plum Fairy, which originally appeared in her pages.

Again, my sincere appreciation to Michael Kinnane of Preston Library, Wembley, for his unfailing interest and assistance.

And last but not least, Becky Osborne, whose help, advice and encouragement I value so much.

COPYRIGHT

As in my previous title, *The Kate Greenaway Doll Book*, there are no copyright restrictions on the patterns in this book, as long as you are planning to produce the bears or dolls or their furniture personally and therefore in limited numbers. The toys in *The Fairytale Doll Book* are a further response to all those readers who have written to me because they wish to sell their work and have asked permission to use my designs.
Both the bear and the doll are specially designed to be quick, easy and inexpensive to make. It is then up to you to decide how much time and money you want to spend on dressing them up.
The patterns are all there for you to choose from –
and you don't have to ask.

British Library Cataloguing in Publication Data

Janitch, Valerie
    The fairytale doll book: introduced by
    the three bears.
    1. Dolls & puppets. Making – Manuals.
    2. Teddy bears. Making – Manuals
    I. Title
    745.592'21

ISBN 0-7153-9183-6 (H/B)
ISBN 0-7153-9857-1 (P/B)

First published 1988
Second impression 1990
First published in paperback 1990

Phototypeset by Typesetters (Birmingham) Ltd,
Smethwick, West Midlands
and printed in The Netherlands
by Smeets Offset BV, Weert
for David & Charles Publishers plc
Brunel House   Newton Abbot   Devon

Distributed in the United States by
Sterling Publishing Co. Inc,
387 Park Avenue South, New York, NY 10016–8810

Details of other books and patterns by
Valerie Janitch can be obtained by writing to her at:
15 Ledway Drive, Wembley Park, Middlesex HA9 9TH.
Please enclose a stamped self-addressed envelope.

Introduction

Fairytales are all about magic and make-believe. There was magic behind every tree the day the Three Bears went down to the woods for their picnic.

This is the story of how Baby Bear met all his favourite storybook characters – when he followed a mysterious brown butterfly deep into the forest, and found a wonderful world of make-believe which you can re-create for yourself or someone you love – just by the magic of threading a needle.

The first part of the book consists of some basic guidelines to help you follow the directions with ease, and to ensure success when you make your own bears, dolls and furniture. Then there are basic patterns for the bears and doll and for basic items of clothing – plus a section on hairstyles.

The INTERESTING part begins on page 30. So why not look there now, and then turn to the Basics for guidance when you have decided which fairytale character you are going to make first.

It all began quite early one morning in Honeysuckle Cottage . . .

Contents

Equipment and Adhesives

Simple, unsophisticated soft toys, such as the ones in this book, need only the most basic sewing equipment, but make sure that the tools in your work-basket are in good condition. Scissors, needles, pins and so on need to be sharp and well aligned. Not only will blunt blades and points produce an unprofessional-looking toy, but they will make your work tedious and difficult. Scissors that make a clean cut and needles which slide smoothly in and out make sewing a pleasure – and enjoyable sewing, like knitting, is a wonderfully soothing way to relax and forget your problems.

Try to have two pairs of scissors: one pair for cutting out and a smaller pair for all the sewing jobs. In addition to ordinary sewing needles (medium to fine, as you like), you will need two tiny safety-pins (or a large tapestry needle) for threading elastic, and a long darning needle for fixing the dolls' hair or sewing on bears' ears. You will find a darning needle useful for other jobs too; it's surprising how often a really long, strong darning needle can solve a problem when all else has failed. A small pair of tweezers can be an enormous help, and pinking shears, although not essential, are very useful.

You will also need a well-sharpened pencil, a ruler, a pair of compasses and some paper-cutting scissors (try to avoid blunting your sewing scissors with paper). A sharp craft knife is another necessary item (see Basics 11). Tracing paper is essential: household greaseproof paper is ideal if you plan to use the patterns only a few times. If you haven't any graph paper, rule a large sheet of plain paper into squares, but make sure that your measurements are absolutely accurate.

Use a clear, all-purpose adhesive: UHU is quick-drying and the long nozzle at the head of the tube makes it extremely easy to use. Use a dry-stick glue to stick fabric to card: some glue-sticks are recommended for use only on paper, so make sure that the one you choose lists fabric as well, such as UHU Stic, which does an excellent job.

Use a PVA adhesive to stick the pieces of corrugated cardboard together for the furniture. When wallpaper paste is specified, any kind of paper paste will do, but wallpaper paste is much cheaper: Polycell Regular is ideal. Wallpaper paste will not adhere to corrugated cardboard with a damp-proof finish; in this case use PVA adhesive.

FOLLOWING THE DIRECTIONS

The instructions are numbered step by step and it is always a good idea to read through the whole of each step, even though it may contain several operations. This will give you a clear picture of what you are aiming to achieve, which will make each stage easier to understand.

MEASUREMENTS

Use either metric or imperial measurements, but *don't* compare the two because they are often different. To make the instructions as simple as possible, each design has been worked out individually in both metric and imperial and the nearest most practical measurement is always given. It is important, therefore, that you use one set of measurements only.

When the direction of measurements is not specifically stated, the depth is given first, followed by the width – ie, 10 × 20cm (4 × 8in) = 10cm (4in) deep × 20cm (8in) wide.

MATERIALS

Most of the items used are widely available, and you may have many of them at home already.

Felt, Fur and Fabric

Never feel guilty if you deliberate for a long time over the choice of fabrics for your toy. Your choice of fabric is the most crucial decision that you have to make because the wrong fur can spoil your cuddly animal, a poor felt can ruin your doll and an unsuitable fabric can make her pretty dress a total disaster.

Fur fabric is not like real fur: look at the back and you will see that it is like a knitted jersey. This allows the fabric to stretch when you stuff it in order to create the smoothly rounded heads and well-fed tummies which are the mark of a truly successful soft toy. It is this secret stretch which makes toys cuddly, so do exploit it to the full and use the stuffing to shape and emphasise all the features which will give your toy its lovable personality.

Felt avoids many problems, like awkward seams, tricky turnings and fraying edges, but it requires careful shopping. Poor quality felt is not worth the thread you use to stitch it, let alone the time spent sewing seams which will pull away when any strain is put on them. Never buy felt which is thin or of an uneven thickness; look for a firm, smooth, even quality, without too much 'fluff' on the surface. A good quality felt will, of course, cost more, but it is money well spent because you will be both frustrated and disappointed if you are tempted to settle for second-best.

If you want to follow the photographs of the dolls, look for a pale flesh-coloured felt. You may find that when you ask for 'flesh' felt, you are shown something very florid which would be fine for a bucolic old colonel with gout, but is quite unsuitable for Cinderella or the Sleeping Beauty. In fact, all the dolls illustrated in this book are made from cream felt, so if you find that the flesh tone is too vivid, look for a rich cream shade instead. (Cream felt is available by mail order from The Handicraft Shop, Northgate, Canterbury CT1 1BE tel: 0227 451188). Failing that, go for the very palest pink you can find. On the other hand, choose a deep coffee-and-cream shade if you want a dark and sultry beauty with jet black hair.

You will always find a suggestion as to the most suitable type of fabric to use for each garment or piece of furniture; for easy identification, the colour shown in the photograph is indicated in the list of materials, but as a general guideline, it is important to avoid thick or knobbly fabrics which are too bulky for items on such a small scale. You will find that thick fabrics are difficult to work with and the results will be disappointing. The same goes for patterned fabrics: a large, bold design which looks wonderful on you will be overpowering on a doll. Tiny floral prints, however, can look enchanting, as do finely checked gingham or a very narrow stripe.

You should also look for a firm, close weave; loosely woven fabrics mean trouble because they fray easily. You will soon find yourself in difficulties if you try to sew small pieces with tiny seams which immediately begin to fray. If you must use a fabric which frays, treat it as the bodice of the Sleeping Beauty's dress (see page 101); the iron-on interlining tends to stiffen the fabric slightly, so bear this in mind – but it will solve the problem.

Never choose stiff fabrics which will stick out unnaturally. Soft fabrics will mould themselves to the figure and the gathers will fall gently and smoothly. When a medium-weight material is recommended, choose a firmly woven cotton-type fabric, like poplin or a polyester-blend summer-dress material. Cotton sheeting is a fraction heavier and is ideal for 'upholstering' the furniture, as will be described later. Fabrics described as 'light-weight' are similar in texture, but thinner and more delicate, like lawn.

Note: Pattern pieces are placed across the width of the fabric for cutting, so that if you are buying fabric, you will need to purchase the smallest possible amount. However, if you are using a piece of fabric that you already have, the width quoted in the list of materials is not always an accepted loom width from selvedge to selvedge, but indicates the actual width of fabric needed.

Patterns and Cutting

Trace the patterns onto household greaseproof paper, or non-woven interlining (Vilene) if you intend to use them often. For pieces that are to be cut in fur fabric or felt, trace those patterns with a fold onto folded paper or interlining; cut through the double thickness then open it out to cut flat in single fur or felt. This precaution also ensures accuracy when you are cutting very small fabric pieces.

To make patterns from the diagrams, place tracing paper over graph paper or rule squares; then use a ruler to measure and rule the lines.

Trace the name of each piece and all the markings onto the pattern, then accurately transfer notches, circles and crosses to the wrong side of the pieces of fabric or felt when you have cut them out.

For patterns that are to be cut in thin card or paper, trace the patterns first onto greaseproof paper, then transfer them to the card. To do this, rub over the back of the tracing paper with a soft pencil, then fix this side flat on your card and retrace the lines with a firm point (ballpoint pen, hard pencil or fine knitting-needle). When you remove the trace, a clear outline should remain on the card. (For patterns that are traced onto folded paper, turn the tracing over and trace your original outline through onto the other side before you open it up.)

Arrows on fabric patterns indicate the straight grain of the fabric – ie, the 'up and down' of the weave. The arrow should be parallel to the selvedge when the pattern is placed on the fabric. Felt pieces may be placed in any direction. Arrows on fur fabric patterns also indicate the direction of the pile.

When a pattern piece is marked 'reverse', you must turn the pattern over to cut the second piece of fabric. Check carefully to ensure that stripes, checks and so on will match equally on both pieces.

Finally, when you cut the felt circles for the bears' or dolls' eyes, it is much easier to cut them accurately if you mark the circle directly onto the felt. Find something with a circular rim the size you require – a thimble, the top from a pill container, pen cap or something similar – but the sharper the edge of the rim, the better. Using a contrasting colour, rub a wax crayon, lead pencil, felt-tip pen or piece of chalk liberally over the rim. Press down onto the felt; then, still pressing the rim down very firmly, twist it, taking great care not to move the position – as if you were using a pastry-cutter. Lift off, and a clearly marked line should remain on the felt. Cut along it with small sharp scissors.

SPECIAL NOTE: BODICE PATTERNS

It is impossible to estimate the exact size of your finished doll as this is influenced by the amount of stretch in your felt – and how enthusiastically you stuff it. The bodice patterns are therefore cut generously to ensure that the garment will fit, even if you are using a fabric that is thicker than recommended. If you want a figure-hugging bodice, on the other hand, it is simple to adjust the fit.

Follow the directions to the point where you have joined the shoulder seams. Now tack the side seams, then try the bodice on your doll (inside out) and pin it to see how much you can take off the sides. Remove the bodice and use your patterns to recut the armhole and side edges in the new position, as shown on the diagram (do not forget the seam allowance).

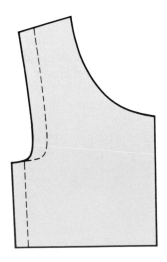

*How to adjust
bodice pattern*

Sewing and Stuffing

Unless stated otherwise, you should always work with the right sides together, 3mm (⅛in) seams are allowed on fabrics (5mm (¼in) on fur). To join felt, oversew the edges very closely, either by hand or by using the satin stitch on your sewing-machine (this makes a very strong seam and looks neat and professional when it is turned to the right side and firmly stuffed).

Use your favourite brand of regular sewing thread for medium-weight fabrics, matching the colour as closely as possible. If you find that your thread breaks, knots or tangles, you may find it helpful to draw it through a block of beeswax before you begin to sew.

In some instances it is necessary to turn the raw edge under when you make a hem – eg, to form a channel to carry elastic. A double hem can be bulky on small garments, however, so where possible turn the hem under only once and then sew it with a herringbone-stitch over the raw edge to prevent it from fraying. In such cases, it will help if you are able to cut your edge along the thread of the fabric.

When you match notches (especially if one side of the fabric or felt is gathered, as for the doll's head, or when you join a skirt to the bodice), it helps to mark each notch on one of the pieces (the gathered side) with a pin, so that the heads extend beyond the edge of the fabric. You can then line up each notch on the other side under a pin-head.

Buy the narrowest round elastic available – but not shirring elastic – and use a tiny safety-pin to thread the elastic through narrow hems for sleeves, waists, ankles and so on. Fix another safety-pin to the other end to prevent it from disappearing.

Careful stuffing is the secret of a professional-looking doll. It isn't difficult, it just needs time and care. Don't try to hurry this stage because, like any well-dressed male or female, the figure inside a smart outfit either sets it off or spoils the effect. Modern stuffings have been developed especially to fill and shape toys properly, giving them the smoothly rounded appearance which is one of the most attractive things about a soft toy, and also ensures a long and healthy life, however much they are loved. Do not try to save money, therefore, by using dangerous foam chips or, even worse, old tights. It is not worth spoiling your doll by economising on stuffing. Top-quality washable polyester is your best choice. Kapok is also satisfactory if you don't mind sneezing all the way through the stuffing stage and then having to brush it out of the carpet afterwards.

The secret of successful stuffing is patience. Use a little stuffing at a time and tease it out so that you are not feeding in solid lumps; then push it well down before you insert the next piece – an unsharpened pencil with an eraser at the end makes a useful tool for small places. This is another occasion when a strong darning needle can prove invaluable: push the needle through the felt to move the stuffing around inside or to pull it into small areas such as dolls' thumbs.

As each area begins to fill up, mould it from the outside with your hands, smoothing and squeezing and rolling it into shape. Make the head smooth and round and emphasise the face especially. Always stuff your doll very firmly, unless the instructions tell you otherwise. An under-stuffed doll can be a disaster because it will tend to get flatter and floppier the more it is cuddled and who wants a doll that hangs its head in shame! If the neck does not hold up firmly, insert a thin stick.

Finishing Touches

As the photographs show, trimmings play an important part in the success of an outfit. As with the fabrics, the trimmings used for the original designs are described in detail in the lists of materials. If you follow these guidelines, therefore, you should have no problems in making the trimmings.

It is a good idea to buy pretty lace edgings and narrow braids when you see them in the shops. Keen doll makers buy any suitable trimmings when they see them and keep them for the day when they turn out to be just what they need for their latest project. Unfortunately, lace and braids seem to be strangely inconsistent in the shops and the wonderful trimming which you noticed a while ago, when you were buying something else, will have disappeared when you return to buy it a few months later.

When you are working on such a small scale, it is important not to use trimmings which are too broad or too heavy for the item they are decorating as they will entirely overpower the finished effect. Do try to follow the widths indicated for the item you are making as they are carefully chosen to complement that particular design (see the relevant illustration). It is usually fairly easy to find lace and beads which are in proportion to a doll of this size, but narrow braids are frequently very hard to come by. Soft-furnishing braids in particular are often stiff and heavy, making them unsuitable for delicate work.

There are two ways around this problem. The first is to find a type of lampshade braid which is, in fact, two very narrow braids joined together down the centre with a silky thread. If you cut through this interlinking thread very carefully, removing the odd bits which remain with a pair of tweezers, you will have two lengths of very narrow braid which is ideal for a doll the size of the one that is featured in this book.

The other alternative is to make your own braid from very narrow ribbon. This means that you can find the perfect colour match or contrast for the garment you are trimming, which adds an extremely professional finish. The method for making your own braid is described in Basics 6.

Ribbon makes a wonderful trimming because it can be used in so many ways. There are no problems with ribbon because the narrowest width is only 1.5mm (¹⁄₁₆in) wide. This very narrow satin ribbon is the one used for the braid described above. Made by Offray, it comes in such a rich palette of colours that your only problem will be deciding which shades to reject. Offray ribbon makes smart little tassels too, while wider versions of the same ribbon make romantic butterfly bows or a selection of realistic roses. All are described in Basics 6.

All the attractive ribbons used for these designs are made by Offray. Where the colour of a ribbon is described with a capital initial letter – eg, Colonial Rose – this is the name of the particular Offray shade that has been used for the item illustrated.

Beads and sequins come in a wide variety of tempting shapes and colours. Avoid them if the toy is for a very small child, but make full use of them when you want a touch of glamour. Shimmering pearls are a particularly effective decoration. You can buy tear-drop pearls as well as round pearls, or they can be purchased in a long string by the metre or yard (but they *won't* scatter all over the floor when you cut the string).

Flowers make a charming trimming for almost any feminine garment. Tiny forget-me-nots or rosebuds can look exquisite on a lacy collar or cap. But beware of blooms which are out of proportion to the figure they are decorating as they will spoil the finished effect. Again, try to buy suitable items when you see them and build up a collection of tiny bunches of flowers, because often you will need only a few heads, seldom the whole bunch. Unfortunately, artificial flowers are not cheap, so try to make a few go a long way, or you could use ribbon roses, as illustrated in the following pages.

Made-to-Match Trimmings

PLAITED BRAID

If you plait 1.5mm ($\frac{1}{16}$in) wide satin ribbon, you can make a very narrow, dainty braid. If you need something wider, use two pieces side by side. The colour range of Offray ribbons is so comprehensive that you can nearly always find just the matching, toning or contrasting shade that you require. You can also plait two or three different shades together, to make a multi-coloured, custom-designed braid to tone with a plain or patterned fabric.

1. The directions for the item that you are making will usually tell you how much ribbon you need to make the length of braid you require. For instance: 'Make a plait from three 25cm (10in) lengths of 1.5mm ($\frac{1}{16}$in) ribbon.' In this case, if you are making the braid in one colour only, cut one 25cm (10in) length of ribbon and one 50cm (20in) length. Fold the longer piece in half, smear a trace of glue inside the fold, place one end of the shorter piece between the fold, then pinch together (figure a).

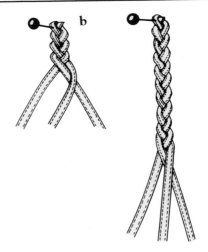

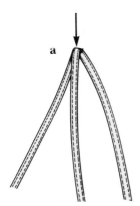

2. Push a pin through the folded end and secure it to a drawing-board or something similar. Then begin to plait very evenly, making sure that the strands of ribbon are always flat – never fold them over. Keep the ribbon taut and draw the plait very firmly between your fingertips every 2–3cm (inch or so) to make it smooth and even (figure b). Hold the ends together with a paper-clip.

3. Glue the braid into place, spreading the glue just beyond the point where you intend to cut it to ensure that it does not unravel. Press the cut ends down well, adding a little more glue if necessary.

4. If you are not following directions, you can calculate the amount of ribbon needed by measuring the length of braid you require and adding a third (then multiply by three for the total amount). For example, if you need a 30cm (12in) length of braid, plait three pieces of ribbon 40cm (16in) long. If you want to make a multi-colour braid in two or three toning shades, divide the total amount by three to calculate the quantity of each ribbon that you will require.

RIBBON BOWS

Although you can simply tie a bow in a piece of ribbon, you will find one of the following two methods far more attractive. The first is excellent for making a formal bow in wide ribbon; the second makes enchanting little butterfly bows.

FORMAL BOWS

1. Fold under the cut ends of your piece of ribbon (the directions will tell you the width and how long it should be), so that they overlap at the centre back (figure a).

2. Gather the centre (figure b) and draw up, binding tightly several times with your thread to hold it securely (figure c).

3. Fold a scrap of ribbon lengthways into three and bind it closely around the centre; secure the ends at the back and trim off the surplus neatly (figure d).

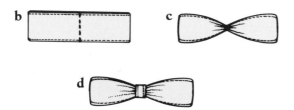

4. Gather across the centre of another piece of ribbon (length again as specified), then draw up tightly and fold it around as figure e for the ties.

5. Stitch the ties behind the bow and trim the cut ends in an inverted V-shape (figure f).

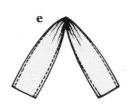

BUTTERFLY BOWS

1. Cut a piece of single-face satin ribbon (the directions will tell you the width and the length). On the wrong side, mark point A at the centre, close to the lower edge (figure g). On the right side, mark dots for points B on the top edge – see your individual directions for the distance points B should be from A. Then trim the cut ends in an inverted V-shape as figure h.

2. Hold the ribbon with the wrong side facing you. Using closely matching thread, bring your needle

through point A from the back, close to the edge of the ribbon. Then curve the ends around and bring the needle through each point B. Draw up so that both points B are over point A (figure i).

3. Make tiny gathering stitches up from points B to C (figure j). Take your thread over the top edge of the bow and gather right down from point C to point D. Draw up neatly, then wind the thread tightly around three or four times and secure at the back so that the result resembles figure k.

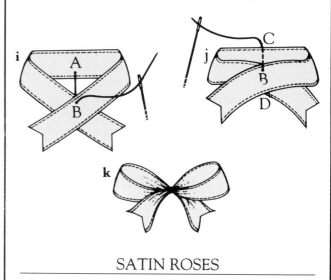

SATIN ROSES

You can make a riot of roses in any size or shape, from bud to full bloom, from appropriately coloured satin ribbons. The width of the ribbon determines the size of the flower: the longer it is, the more petals it will have. The directions will indicate the width and length that you should use for each design, although you will soon be able to judge this for yourself. Use single-face satin ribbon (except for miniature 3mm (⅛in) roses) and matching thread.

1. Cut a length of ribbon as directed. Fold the corner as the broken line on figure a and bring point A down to meet points B as figure b. Fold

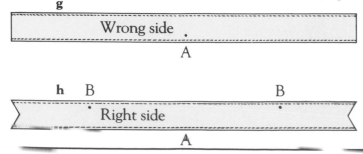
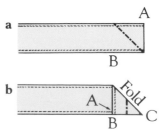

again as the broken line on figure b and bring point C over point A to meet point B as figure c. (Omit the second fold for 3mm (⅛in) ribbon.)

2. Now roll the ribbon around about four turns, with the folded corner inside, to form a tight tube, and make a few stitches through the base to hold (figure d). This forms the centre of the rose.

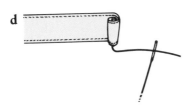

3. To make the petals, fold the ribbon down so that the edge is aligned with the tube (figure e), then curve the ribbon around the tube to form a cone, keeping the top of the tube level with the

diagonal fold. When the tube again lies parallel to the remaining ribbon, make two or three stitches at the base to hold the petal you have just made (figure f).

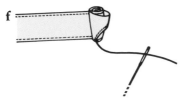

4. Continue to make petals with the remainder of the ribbon, sewing each one to the base of the flower before you start the next (figure g). Shape the rose as you work by gradually making the petals a little more open.

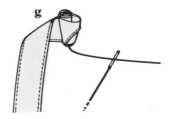

5. Finish the cut end neatly underneath the base of the completed rose (figure h).

TINY TASSELS

1. Take a length of 1.5mm (⅟₁₆in) wide ribbon and fold it as instructed – the length and number of folds determine the size of the tassel. Your individual directions will tell you how much ribbon and how many lengths you will require.

2. Hold the folded ends neatly together and absolutely level (figure a), then make a knot at the centre (figure b). Take the two sides down so that

all the ends are together, then bind very tightly with matching thread close under the knot (figure c).

3. Snip off the folded ends and trim neatly to the length required (figure d).

Big Bears and Little Bears

Mother Bear, Father Bear, Baby Bear and Goldilocks are all made in exactly the same way. Mother and Father Bear are identical (except for their noses) and are 44cm (17in) high. Baby Bear is only 31cm (12in) high. Goldilocks is a little bigger than Baby Bear, so take care to lengthen the body, arm and leg as indicated on the pattern pieces and copy the name of the character onto each piece for easy identification. The Bear family are all made up in a deep golden fur fabric, but Goldilocks is a soft honey-blonde colour (photo page 108).

MATERIALS

60cm (¾yd) fur fabric, 75cm (30in) wide, for either Mother Bear or Father Bear
or 40cm (½yd) fur fabric, 75cm (30in) wide, for either Baby Bear or Goldilocks
Scraps of black felt
Polyester stuffing
Matching and black sewing threads
Stranded black embroidery cotton
Stiff card (double-thickness cereal carton)
Clear adhesive

Patterns: See Basics 3 for general notes. Remember, arrows indicate straight of fabric and also the direction of the pile. You may find it helpful to trace a pattern for every piece of fur fabric that you need to cut – ie, two heads (reversing the second), four arms (reversing two), and so on. Pin the pattern pieces to the wrong side of your fur fabric and cut the back of the fabric with small pointed scissors, avoiding cutting through the pile as well.
Note: 5mm (¼in) seams are allowed. Work with the right sides together unless otherwise indicated. Pin seams before stitching, pushing any protruding pile down between the two layers of fabric. When you turn to the right side, release any pile that is caught in the seam by brushing it very firmly with a pin. Do not clip seams before turning.

1. Check that you have the correct pieces for the character you want. Cut the head twice (reverse the second piece) and the gusset once. Cut the body, the leg and the sole twice each and the seat once. Cut the arm four times (reversing two pieces) and cut the ear four times (note the direction of the pile). Cut the sole twice more in card, slightly smaller, as indicated by the broken line. Mark notches and circles. Leave head pattern pinned to fabric.

2. For the Three Bears only (not Goldilocks), first mark the mouth very carefully on each head-piece. To do this, stick a pin straight down through the pattern and fabric every 3mm (⅛in) or so. Push the heads right down against the paper, then gently ease the pattern away to leave the pins stuck in the fabric. Using black sewing thread, back-stitch along this line, following the position of the pins very accurately and removing them as you sew (make sure that your stitches show clearly on the right side).

3. Join the two head-pieces between points A–B. Very carefully match the tip of the gusset (A) to the top of the seam; then join to each side of the head between points A–C. Join dart (E–D). Turn to the right side.

4. Join the two body pieces at each shoulder (F–G). Mark the centre front and back of the neck edge. Push the head inside the body and pin, matching point B to centre front of neck, point D to centre back, and points F to notches on head. Stitch securely across the back (between F–F). Gather across the front edge of the head (as indicated). Pin evenly to the body and draw up to fit. Stitch securely. Turn head to the wrong side again.

5. Join each pair of arm pieces from the top to the notch (G–H), then join to the body, matching circles and points G. Join the rest of the arm seam (between point H and the circle). Then join the sides of the body.

6. Join the top edge of the seat to the lower edge of the body back. Then turn under a narrow hem along the lower edges of the seat and the body front. Turn to the right side.

7. Join the centre front seam of each leg between points J–K. Fit the sole around the lower edge of the foot, matching points K and L. Stitch together. Turn to the right side and push the card down into the sole (pin temporarily from the outside into the cut edge of the card to hold it in place).

8. Stuff the head firmly and evenly to emphasise the shaping and to ensure that it is nicely rounded.

Make sure that the sides are well filled and, when you have finished, push a little extra stuffing into the front between the nose and the chin. Mould the area with your hands, holding the head up and looking straight at the face to make sure that the head is a good shape.

Stuff the arms and then the upper half of the body, pushing well up into the neck. Stuff the legs firmly, pushing well down into the feet. Pin the centre front seam (J) to centre back (M), then stitch across the top.

9. Mark the centre front on the lower edge of the body, and the centre back on the lower edge of the seat. Pin the front edge of the body over the top of the legs (feet forward), positioning each between the side and the centre. Stitch firmly into place. Oversew the edges of the body front and the seat firmly together at the centre, then pin the lower edge of the seat over the top of one leg and stitch into place. Complete stuffing the body (but not so full that the animal is unable to sit down); then

stitch the seat over the top of the second leg.

10. For each ear, oversew two pieces together all round, leaving the straight lower edge open. Make a narrow hem around this edge. Turn to the right side. Join the lower edges with a gathering stitch and draw up into a softly curved shape. Pin and then stitch firmly to the sides of the head: the inner corner of each ear should be level with the gusset seam.

11. For the Three Bears, embroider the mouth in stem stitch over the previously marked line, using six strands of embroidery cotton. Cut the eyes and nose in black felt. Pin to the head, moving them about until you are satisfied with the bear's expression. Mark the position of each eye with pins, then remove the felt and carefully snip away the fur beneath. Glue the eye into place. Glue the nose on in the same way. Very carefully trim off any excess fur around the eyes and mouth, but do so only a little at a time to avoid snipping off too much.

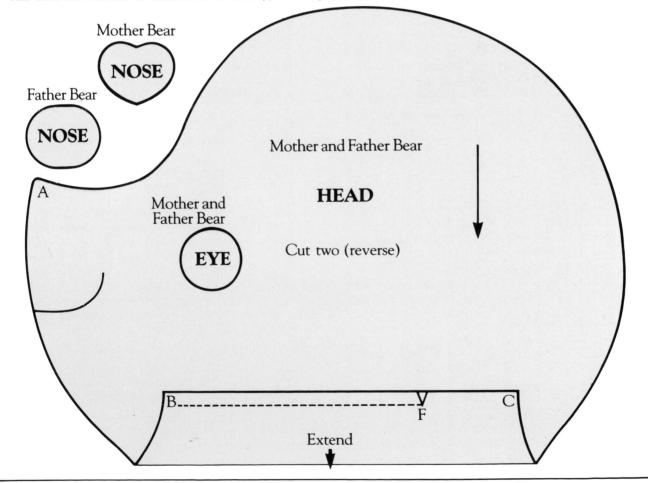

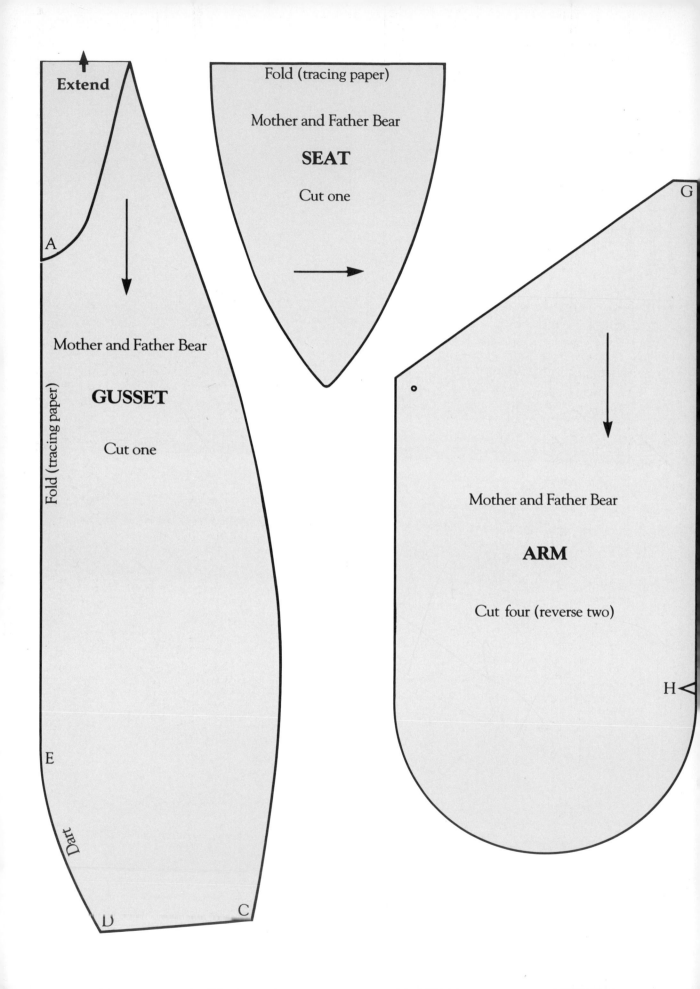

Extend

A

Fold (tracing paper)

Mother and Father Bear

GUSSET

Cut one

E

Dart

D

C

Fold (tracing paper)

Mother and Father Bear

SEAT

Cut one

G

Mother and Father Bear

ARM

Cut four (reverse two)

H

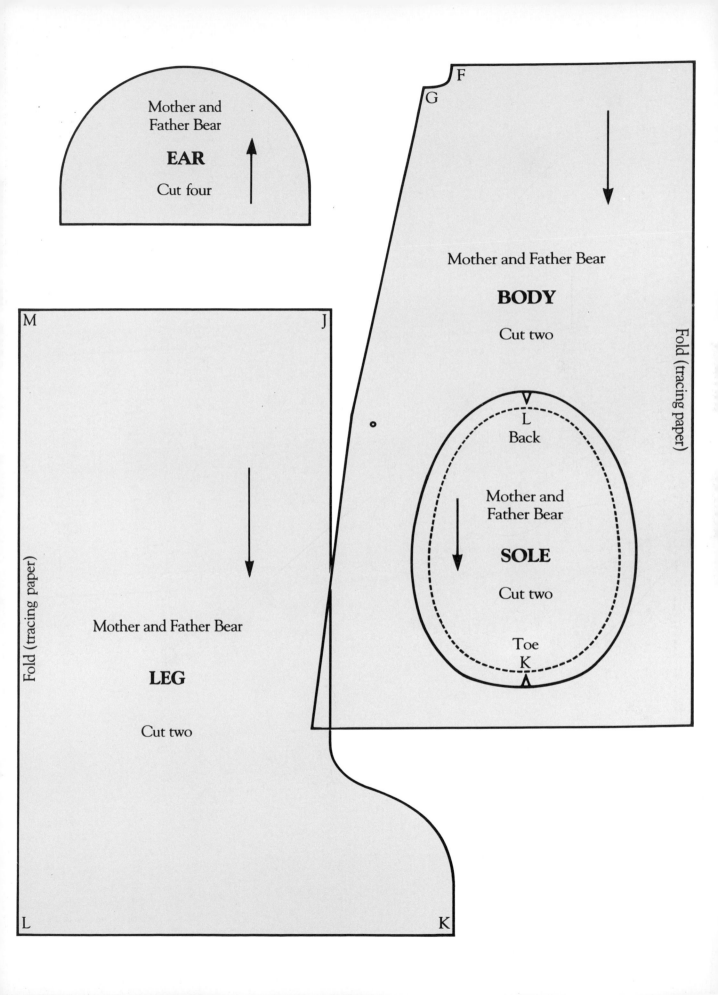

Mother and
Father Bear

EAR

Cut four

F

G

Mother and Father Bear

BODY

Cut two

Fold (tracing paper)

M   J

L
Back

Mother and
Father Bear

SOLE

Cut two

Mother and Father Bear

LEG

Cut two

Toe
K

Fold (tracing paper)

L   K

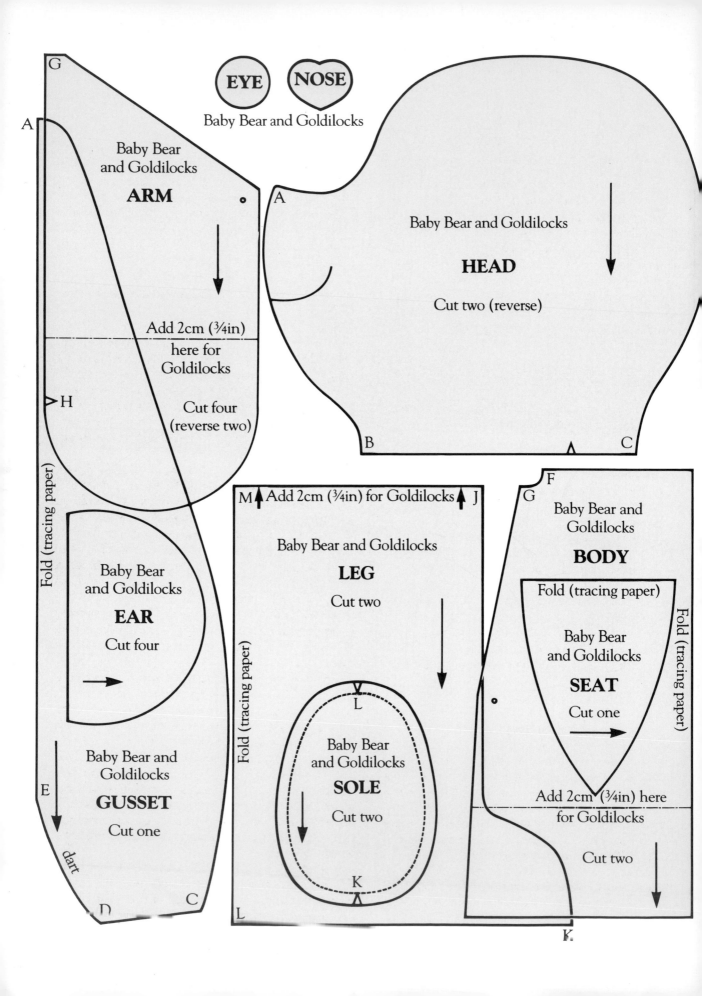

The Fairytale Doll

Accuracy in cutting and in transferring and matching the markings is vital if your doll is to look good. Felt has a certain amount of stretch and this will become evident when the doll is stuffed, so always place the arm and leg patterns in the same direction. (The worst thing you can do is to cut one arm or leg along the direction of the 'stretch' and the second one across it because this will result in one long, thin arm or leg and one short and fat.) Oversew the edges closely to join the felt.

MATERIALS

Check the list of materials for the doll you are making to see which of the following items you will need:

Three 30cm (12in) squares of flesh felt
or two squares of flesh plus one 30cm (12in) square in contrast felt for the legs
Knitting yarn for the hair

1. Polyester stuffing
2. Scrap of black felt, for eyes
3. 2 domed coloured sequins, 8mm (5/16in) in diameter, for eyes
4. 2 domed black sequins, 5mm (3/16in) in diameter, for pupils
5. Stranded deep pink embroidery cotton
6. Matching and black sewing threads
7. Thin stick, 15cm (6in) long (optional)
8. Scrap of stiff card (or margarine-tub lid)
9. Clear adhesive

1. Cut the head front and back and the body front and back once each. Cut the leg and sole twice each. Cut the arm four times, reversing two. It is helpful to cut the first two arms, then turn the pieces over and pin them to the felt to cut the second two, keeping the cut edges absolutely level and leaving them pinned together for sewing. Mark notches carefully. Cut the sole twice more in stiff card, slightly smaller, as broken line.
2. Gather across lower edge of front head, between x's. Pin to top edge of body front, draw up to fit, then oversew the head and neck together. Join the back head to the body back in the same way.

3. Gather close to edge of front head between o's. Pin head-pieces right sides together, matching x's and notches. Draw up to fit, distributing the gathers evenly between the notches, then join all round, leaving the straight neck edge open between x's.
4. Join the side edges of the body, below x's, stiching especially securely around the neck. Turn to the right side.
5. Stuff head very firmly, working slowly and carefully, moulding it into a smoothly rounded shape. When you think you have finished, push a little more stuffing into each side of the lower part of the face (the jawline) to resemble a round apple – not an upside-down pear. You can stiffen the neck by pushing a thin stick up the body into the head: then complete stuffing the neck and body around it.
6. Join two pieces for each arm, leaving the space between the notches open. Make tiny stitches, close together, around the hand and thumb (if you are sewing by machine, stitch only as far as the arrows, then sew around the thumb by hand). Turn to the right side, stuff firmly and close the seam. Begin by stuffing the thumb, pushing in just a little filling with the points of your smallest scissors (but take care), then draw it up to the tip with a darning needle from the outside. When the stuffing is completed, use your darning needle again to ease the filling in the hand over to join the top of the thumb.
7. Fold each leg in half, as pattern, and join the centre front seam between the top and toe. Fit the sole inside the lower edge, matching notches to front seam (toe) and centre back of leg. Stitch together. Turn to the right side. Fit the card sole inside and hold in place temporarily with pins pushed through felt into cut edge of card. Stuff the leg firmly, then pin top edges together, matching x's so that centre front seam meets centre back of leg, folding at each side as indicated by the broken line. Gather across the top and draw up to measure 4.5cm (1¾in).
8. Pin the legs side by side and toes forward, to the inside of the body front (check feet are level). Stitch securely. Pin lower edge of body back over legs level with front stitching line. Join across one

leg, then complete stuffing the body before sewing the other leg.

9. Using double thread and following the dots on the pattern, sew the tops of the arms securely to the shoulders to allow free movement in all directions. Make 1cm (⅜in) stitches through the inside arm, taking your needle in at one dot and out through the other, joining to the shoulder with stitches through from front to back, following the dots on the body patterns. Then finish by sewing the centre top of the arm seam to the point of the shoulder, pulling the thread taut.

Note: To make elbow or knee joints, stitch through the stuffed limbs, drawing your (double) thread very tight, at the same time easing the stuffing away from the joint.

Now turn to Basics 9 for your doll's hairstyle. When you have completed the hair, return to step 10 of this section to make the features – unless you are instructed otherwise in the directions for the doll concerned.

10. Cut the eye twice in black felt. Place a black sequin on top of a coloured one and stitch both in the centre of the felt with six straight stitches in black thread to form a star. (If the doll is for a very small child, omit the sequins and embroider just a star with straight stitches in the centre of a coloured felt circle.) Pin the eyes to the face to determine their position – about 8cm (3in) below centre top of head (seam). Reposition the eyes several times until you are sure that they are in the correct place.

11. Using black thread, make three straight stitches 3mm (⅛in) long in the same place, for the nose. Position the stitches level with the bottom of the eyes.

12. Sketch out the shape of the mouth with tiny pins, about 1cm (⅜in) below the nose. Experiment with wide curves or small semi-circles, depending whether you want a broad grin or a shy, demure smile. Wait until your doll is looking back at you with just the expression you want – then capture the line in stem stitch with three strands of embroidery cotton, removing the pins as you work and using the holes for guidance.

13. Glue the eyes in place.

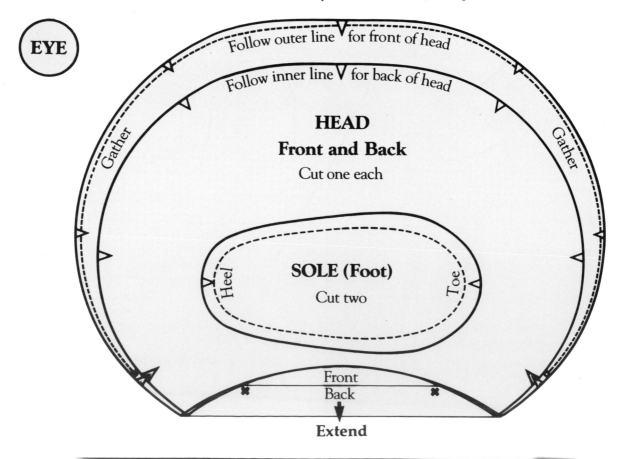

EYE

Follow outer line for front of head

Follow inner line for back of head

Gather

Gather

HEAD
Front and Back
Cut one each

Heel

SOLE (Foot)
Cut two

Toe

Front
Back

Extend

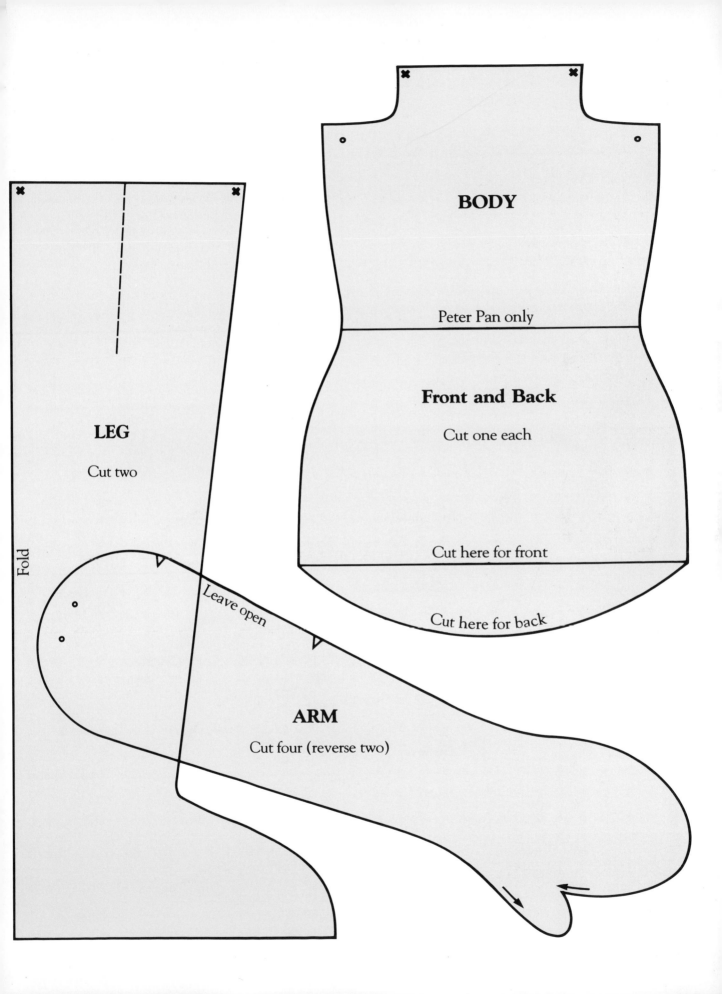

BODY

Peter Pan only

Front and Back

Cut one each

Cut here for front

Cut here for back

LEG

Cut two

Fold

Leave open

ARM

Cut four (reverse two)

Hairstyles

The hair is made by stitching small 'skeins' of yarn over the head. Then add a bun, a plait, a top-knot, a pony-tail, bunches of curls – the styling possibilities are endless.

To make a skein, cut a piece of stiff card 8–10cm (3–4in) wide by the depth specified in the directions for the doll you are making. Wind the yarn smoothly and evenly around the card the number of times stated (more if your yarn is thinner, less if it is thicker).

For a smooth, sleek hairstyle, tie the loops tightly at each edge with a 20cm (8in) length of yarn (figure 1). Slip the skein off the card and tie the centre, either loosely or tightly, as directed (figure 2).

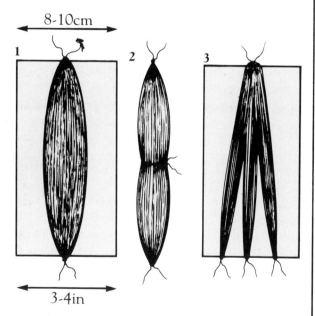

8-10cm

3-4in

For loose hair, fringes and so on, the skeins will be tied at the centre only and fixed in different ways, but this is clearly set out in the individual directions and the method is always only a variation on the basic skein described above.

Use matching double thread and a long darning needle to stitch the skein to the head, and spread a little glue underneath the yarn to hold it in place. Trim off neatly the centre ties and loose ends of the yarn.

To make a plait, wind the yarn the specified number of times around a piece of card exactly as

above, but tie the loops tightly together at the top edge only. Divide the strands at the bottom edge into three and tie each group separately (figure 3). Slip the yarn off the card and plait the three sections neatly together. Consult the directions for the doll you are making to see how the bottom of the plait should be finished off.

ALICE

1st two skeins: Wind yarn twenty times around a 20cm (8in) deep card. Tie tightly at one edge only. Stitch the tied sections of the skeins to the centre back of the head, side by side, 2.5cm (1in) apart and 1.5cm (⅝in) below the seam (circles, figure 4) to hang down as figure 5.

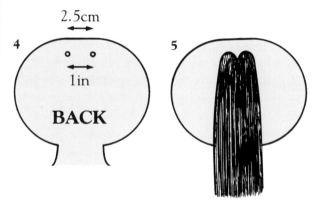

2.5cm

1in

BACK

2nd skein: Wind yarn twenty times around a 30cm (12in) deep card. Tie quite loosely at one edge only with a contrast yarn. Place this skein over the top of the head so that the loops hang down the back (over the 1st two skeins) and the tied section overlaps the face 7–8cm (3in). Spread the skein out over the seam to cover 3cm (1¼in) and stitch tautly over the strands to hold them in place, taking your thread across several times between points A–A (figure 6).
3rd two skeins: Wind yarn twenty times around a 28cm (11in) deep card. Tie as for the 2nd skein. Place each over the seam, as for the previous skein, covering 2cm (¾in) at each side of it. Stitch into place as for the 2nd skein, between points B–A and A–B (figure 6).
4th two skeins: Wind yarn thirty times around the

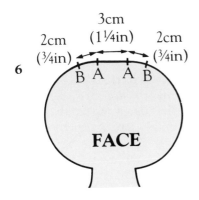

20cm (8in) deep card. Tie tightly at one edge (as for the 1st two skeins). Stitch the tied section over the seam at point B (figure 6), close against the 3rd skeins, to hang down each side of the head.

5th two skeins: Wind yarn twenty times around the 20cm (8in) deep card. Tie as for the 1st two skeins. Stitch the tied section directly in front of, and against, the 4th skeins.

Spread glue lightly all over the head and also under the upper part of the fringe (in front of the seam), then press the hair down to hold it in place.

Stitch one end of blue ribbon under the hair at the nape of the neck, then bring it up through the middle of the 5th skein at one side, across the top of the head to cover the stitches, then down through the middle of the 5th skein at the other side and round to the back again. Stitch securely at nape of neck and trim off any surplus.

Remove the contrast ties and cut through the loops all the way round. Trim neatly to length, shaping the fringe across the face as illustrated.

THE MAD HATTER

Note: The yarn used for the doll illustrated was a slightly fluffy, Shetland-type wool, a little thinner than most double-knits. This meant that it was necessary to wind it around the card thirty times to give the Mad Hatter his rather wild and hairy head of hair. However, if you are using an ordinary double-knit wool, you may find twenty-five times will give you a sufficiently thick skein. Judge for yourself when you see how well the skeins cover the head. If, when you reach the end, you feel that the hair is not thick enough, just add another small skein at the back, then spread the previous skeins out and glue them to the head as described below.

1st skein: Wind yarn 25–30 times around a 20cm (8in) deep card. Slide off carefully and tie the centre loosely. Place centrally across the top of the head ends hanging down at each side, so that the tied centre of the skein is level with the seam at the back and overlaps the front head 2.5cm (1in) (between points A–B on figure 7). Stitch the centre with matching thread, removing the tie as you do so.

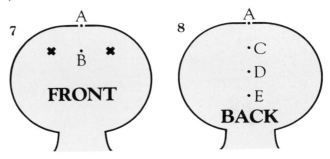

2nd skein: Wind yarn 25–30 times around a 25cm (10in) deep card. Slide off and tie as before. Position directly behind the first skein, covering 2.5cm (1in) at the centre top of the back head (between points A–C on figure 8). Stitch into position in the same way.

3rd skein: Make as for the 2nd skein, positioning so that the centre covers 2.5cm (1in) below the previous skein (between points C–D on figure 8).

4th skein: Prepare yarn as for 1st skein, then stitch behind the 3rd skein so that the centre covers 2.5cm (1in) as before (between points D–E on figure 8).

Cut all the loops, then catch a few of the loose front strands to the head, 3cm (1¼in) each side of the centre (the points marked with an X on figure 7), so that they do not fall down over the forehead.

When you have made the Mad Hatter's shirt, and his wing collar and bow-tie are in position, spread glue all over the head and press the hair firmly down, arranging it so that it is evenly distributed. Trim the cut ends neatly all round.

CLARA

Note: Use glue only if you feel that it is necessary (possibly under the 3rd and 4th skeins). Leave the centres of the skeins pinned to the head as described, until they are all in place.

1st skein: Wind yarn twenty times around a 22cm (8¾in) deep card. Tie tightly at both edges, then loosely around the centre. Place across the front of the doll's head and pin the tied centre so that it covers 2cm (¾in) in front of the seam. Take the two ends smoothly down at each side and stitch them over the seam (figures 9 and 10).

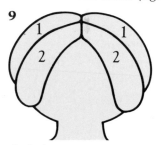
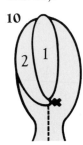

2nd skein: Prepare as for 1st skein. Pin the centre immediately in front of the first skein to cover another 2cm (¾in) of the forehead. Take the ends down at each side and pin them over the seam, just below the ends of the 1st skein (figures 9 and 10). Do not stitch into position until you have completed the next step.

Looped plaits: Make as directed at beginning of the chapter (see page 22), winding the yarn fifteen times around a 15cm (6in) deep card for each plait. Catch the ends together at the bottom of the plait, removing the ties, then loop round and stitch the two ends of the plait together. Stitch the top of the loop immediately behind the pinned end of the 2nd skein, against the seam. Remove the pin so that you can stitch, if more convenient, then stitch the ends of the 2nd skein into position.

3rd skein: Prepare as for 1st skein, but tie the centre tightly. Pin the centre to the back of the head immediately behind the 1st skein, then take the ends down and stitch them over the top of the looped plait at each side.

4th skein: Make a skein, winding the yarn twenty times around a 20cm (8in) deep card and tying the centre tightly. Pin the centre immediately behind the previous skein, then take the ends down and stitch them to the head alongside the ends of that skein.

5th skein: Make a similar skein, winding the yarn twenty times around a 17cm (6¾in) deep card. Pin the centre and stitch the ends exactly as described for the 4th skein.

6th skein: Make a similar skein, winding the yarn twenty times around a 15cm (6in) deep card. Pin the centre and stitch the ends in the same way so

that the ends are together at the nape of the neck. Finish all the ends neatly across the back of the neck.

This amount of yarn should cover the head very adequately. If it does not, add one or more skeins, as necessary.

Stitch over the top of the head, removing the centre ties as you go, to form a centre parting.

THE SUGAR PLUM FAIRY

1st skein: Wind yarn ten times around a 30cm (12in) deep card. Tie tightly at both edges and then loosely around the centre. Pin centre to middle of forehead so that the front edge is 4cm (1½in) in front of the seam (figure 11). Take each half of the skein down across the face, around the sides of the head (as illustrated) and across the back, pinning the ends to meet at the nape of the neck (figure 12).

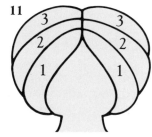
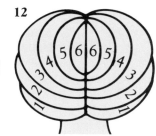

2nd skein: Prepare as for 1st skein. Pin centre close to previous skein, then take each half smoothly around to the back so that it rests close above the 1st skein, pinning the ends as before (figures 11 and 12).

3rd skein: Wind yarn ten times around a 28cm (11in) deep card and tie as above. Pin to the head as for 2nd skein (figures 11 and 12). These three skeins should cover the front head, the back edge of the 3rd skein level with the seam at the centre top (figure 11).

With matching thread, stitch across the centre of the three skeins three or four times, drawing the thread tight and removing the pins and centre ties. One by one, beginning with the 1st skein, lift one side and spread glue on the head underneath, then replace, pressing down into position. At the back, when both sides are complete, join the two ends by knotting the ties together tightly, then stitch neatly over the joined ends. When all three skeins are fixed in this way, complete covering the rest of the head.

4th skein: Wind yarn ten times around a 23cm (9in) deep card. Tie tightly at sides and centre. Stitch centre to top of head over the seam, close behind 3rd skein. Take the sides down over back of the head, positioning close against the previous skein. Glue, tie and stitch as before (figure 12).

5th skein: Wind yarn ten times around a 17cm (6¾in) deep card and tie as for the 4th skein. Fix to the head in the same way, close to the previous skein (figure 12).

6th skein: Wind yarn ten times around a 13cm (5in) deep card and tie as last two skeins. Fix to the head in the same way.

These six skeins should cover the head very adequately. If they do not, add another skein to fill the remaining area.

Wind the yarn thirty times around a 15cm (6in) deep card to make a loose plait (see page 22) and stitch the ends together at the bottom. Fix down back of the head to cover ends of the skeins, stitching top of plait to centre top of head and bottom at the nape of the neck.

To make her top-knot, wind the yarn twenty times around a 23cm (9in) card. Tie at both ends and slide off. Make a loose knot at the centre of the skein, then knot the ties together underneath. Stitch to the top of head, immediately in front of the plait.

THE TOY SOLDIER PRINCE

Mark the front head with pins, as shown in figure 13. Point A is central, 3cm (1¼in) below the seam: the points marked X are each 4cm (1½in) from point A, and 3cm (1¼in) in front of the seam.

Make skeins as described, but tie only at the centre.

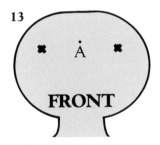

1st skein: Wind yarn twenty times around a 28cm (11in) deep card: slide off carefully and tie the centre loosely. Pin centrally across the top of the head, over the seam, with the ends hanging down

at each side, the tied centre covering 1cm (⅜in) each side of the seam.

2nd skein: Wind yarn twenty times around a 25cm (10in) deep card. Tie the centre loosely. Pin to the front head so that the centre covers 2cm (¾in) between the 1st skein and point A. Stitch across both skeins with matching thread, removing the ties and pins as you do so.

3rd skein: Wind yarn twenty times around a 25cm (10in) deep card again, but this time tie the centre tightly. Stitch the centre to the back of the head, behind the 1st skein.

4th skein: Wind yarn twenty times around a 23cm (9in) deep card and tie the centre tightly. Stitch behind the 3rd skein to cover the back of the head (if it does not, add another skein as necessary).

Cut all the loops, then catch the front strands to the head at each side by stitching over them between the point marked X and the seam. Spread the glue over the rest of the head and press the hair firmly down, arranging it so that the head is evenly covered. When the doll is dressed and the helmet is fixed in position, trim the cut ends neatly all round.

CINDERELLA

1st two skeins: Follow the directions for Alice (see page 22).

2nd skein: Follow the directions for Alice, but wind the yarn thirty times around the card and spread it out to cover 5cm (2in).

3rd skein: Wind yarn thirty times around a 23cm (9in) deep card. Tie one edge loosely, then cut the other edge: open it out and place across the (back) head, the cut ends hanging down equally at each side. Pin the tied centre to cover an area of 2cm (¾in) behind the seam.

4th skein: Prepare as for 3rd skein and pin the centre close against the previous skein to cover 2cm (¾in) in front of the seam.

5th skein: Prepare as for 3rd skein, but wind the yarn around a 20cm (8in) deep card, and pin the centre to cover 2cm (¾in) in front of the 4th skein.

Stitch right across the tied centres several times with matching thread, then remove the ties.

Lift the hair and spread glue lightly over the head, then press the hair down to hold it in place.

Trim the cut ends to length all round, then cut the front loops and trim the fringe to shape.

THE FAIRY GODMOTHER

Follow the directions for the Sugar Plum Fairy (see page 24), but at the end, omit the top-knot and make a fuller plait by winding the yarn around a 20cm (8in) deep card.

HANSEL

Stick pins into the head as shown in figure 14. Point A is central and over the seam; points B are each 2cm (¾in) from point A, and points C are 2cm (¾in) from point B.

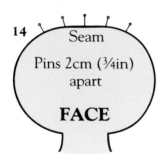

14 Seam

Pins 2cm (¾in) apart

FACE

1st two skeins: Wind the yarn twenty-five times around a 25cm (10in) deep card. Remove carefully and tie the skein loosely 8cm (3¼in) from one end. Place over the head with the tie between points A–B, the shorter end overlapping the face. Cut all the loops.

2nd two skeins: Prepare as for the 1st two skeins, but wind the yarn around a 28cm (11in) deep card and tie 12cm (4¾in) from one end then place the tie over the head as before between points B–C.

Stitch securely over the skeins between points C–C, removing the ties.

Lift the hair and spread glue all over the head, then press down to hold the under-hair firmly in place.

Trim the cut ends neatly all round.

GRETEL

Stick pins into the face as shown in figure 15. Point A is central and 5cm (2in) below the seam; point B is 3.5cm (1⅜in) below point A; points C are level with point B and 4cm (1½in) away from it; points D are a little higher than point C and 2.5cm (1in) away. The distance between point B and the neck seam should not be less than about

3.5cm (1⅜in). If it *is* less, simply raise the pins a fraction to compensate.

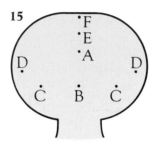

15

1st skein: Wind yarn thirty times around an 18cm (7in) deep card. Tie the loops loosely at one edge, then cut the loops across the other edge and open out. Stick pin E 2cm (¾in) above pin A, then pin the centre of the skein to cover the area between these two pins. Take the two sides down and catch them to the face, taking your thread between pins C–D.

2nd skein: Wind yarn thirty times around a 20cm (8in) deep card. Tie and cut as for the 1st skein. Stick pin F 2cm (¾in) above pin E, then pin the centre of the skein between these two pins.

3rd skein: Wind yarn thirty times around a 23cm (9in) deep card. Tie and cut as for 1st skein. Stick a pin 2cm (¾in) above pin F (1cm (⅜in) behind the seam), then pin the centre of the skein between the two pins.

4th skein: Prepare as for the 2nd skein, but tie the centre tightly. Then pin immediately behind the previous skein.

5th skein: Wind yarn thirty times around a 19cm (7½in) deep card. Tie and cut as for the 4th skein and pin close behind it.

Add another skein, if necessary to cover the back of the head.

Stitch securely over the centres of all the skeins to hold in position, removing the ties.

Glue to the head to hold in position, but as you do so, spread a little glue over the hair between pins C–D, then bring the second skein down over it and press firmly into place.

Trim the cut ends neatly all round.

LITTLE RED RIDING HOOD

Follow the directions for the Sugar Plum Fairy (see page 24), but make a shorter plait by winding the yarn round a 10cm (4in) deep card and omit the top-knot.

To make each curl, wind the wool ten times around the tip of your forefinger, then catch all the loops together at one point with matching thread. Remove from your finger. Make twelve curls and stitch to the head as indicated by the points marked X on figure 16:

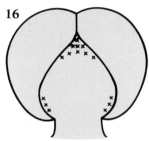

16

One curl at the centre top of the forehead
Three curls just below
Five curls in a slight curve just below the second row
Three curls at each side of the face.

PETER PAN

Follow the directions for Hansel's hair.

WENDY

Follow the directions for Cinderella's hair (see page 25).

THE SLEEPING BEAUTY

Follow the directions for Gretel's hair, then make a top-knot as directed for the Sugar Plum Fairy (see page 25) and stitch to the crown of the head.

PRINCE FLORIMUND

Follow the directions for Hansel's hair.

Petticoats, Pantalettes, Panties, Trousers, Breeches and Shoes

These garments are all basically the same throughout the book, but with variations for each individual doll. Study the directions for the doll you are making to see the amounts that you will require and any individual instructions for that particular garment. You can then use the basic pattern and directions.
Note: When dressing a female doll, you will find it easier to put the pantalettes on first, followed by the dress (feet first) and then her petticoat.

PETTICOAT

1. Cut a strip the depth required (see below), right across the width of the fabric.
2. Join the two side edges to form a centre back seam. Turn under the raw top edge and then make a 1cm (⅜in) hem. Thread the elastic through and draw up to fit waist.
3. Fit petticoat on doll and turn up hem to the required length, then stitch. Trim lower edge as required.

ALICE: See the individual directions for this doll.
CINDERELLA: Cut the fabric 25cm (10in) deep. When complete, fit on the doll but don't turn up the hem until it is fully dressed because then you will be able to determine the length of the petticoat in relation to the underskirt of the dress.
FAIRY GODMOTHER: Cut the fabric 28cm (11in) deep.
GRETEL: Cut the yellow fabric 23cm (9in) deep.

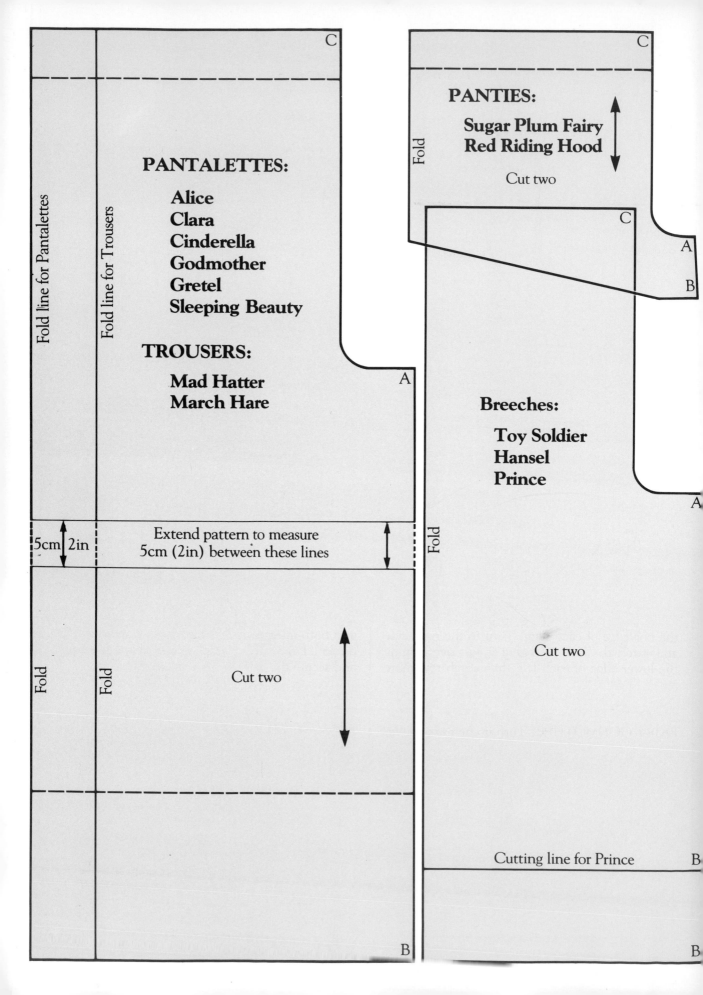

C

Fold line for Pantalettes

Fold line for Trousers

PANTALETTES:

Alice
Clara
Cinderella
Godmother
Gretel
Sleeping Beauty

TROUSERS:

Mad Hatter
March Hare

A

5cm | 2in

Extend pattern to measure
5cm (2in) between these lines

Fold

Fold

Cut two

B

C

PANTIES:

Sugar Plum Fairy
Red Riding Hood

Cut two

Fold

C

A

B

Fold

Breeches:

Toy Soldier
Hansel
Prince

A

Cut two

Cutting line for Prince

B

B

Fit the petticoat on the doll so that the waist elastic rests on her hips.

RED RIDING HOOD: Cut the fabric 18cm (7in) deep. Don't complete the petticoat until the dress is finished, then fit it on the doll with the dress on top and turn up the hem so that it is a fraction above that of the skirt. Trim with lace over the stitching line.

SLEEPING BEAUTY: Cut the fabric 28cm (11in) deep. Trim the lower edge with a double row of cream lace.

PANTALETTES

1. Cut the pattern twice.
2. Fold each piece in half (as pattern) and join the side seam A–B. With right sides together, join the two pieces between points A and C for centre front and back seams. Clip curve and press seam open.
3. Turn under the raw top edge and then make a 1cm (3⁄8in) hem, as indicated by the broken line. Thread the elastic through and draw up to fit waist.
4. Fit on doll and turn up leg hems as below. Trim to match the petticoat.

ALICE: Make a 3.5cm (1⅜in) deep hem around the lower edge of each leg (see broken line). Then make another line of stitching 5mm (¼in) below the first one. Thread the elastic through the channels and draw up to fit the legs.

CLARA: Fit on doll and turn up hems to ankle-length (see photograph). Herringbone-stitch over the raw edge of each hem. Turn to the right side and stitch the lace so that it is just overlapping the lower edge of each leg; then stitch two more rows of lace above the first one, each about 5mm (¼in) apart.

CINDERELLA: Follow the directions for Alice.

FAIRY GODMOTHER: Turn up hems to ankle-length, then stitch.

GRETEL: Follow the directions for Alice.

SLEEPING BEAUTY: Turn up the hems to ankle-length. Trim with a double row of cream lace.

PANTIES

1. Using the Panties pattern, follow steps 1, 2 and 3 for making Pantalettes (see above). *Note:* If you are using satin (for instance, for the Sugar Plum Fairy), take care to avoid fraying when you clip the seams; if this occurs, seal the cut edges with a smear of adhesive.

SUGAR PLUM FAIRY: Bind the edge of each leg, then stitch lace on top of binding.

LITTLE RED RIDING HOOD: Turn under a very narrow hem round the edge of each leg, then stitch lace on top.

FABRIC TROUSERS

1. Follow the directions for making Pantalettes (note fold line and remember to match checks or stripes carefully). Herringbone stitch over the raw edges of the leg hems.

FELT BREECHES

1. Cut the pattern piece twice in felt.
2. Fold each piece in half (as pattern) and oversew the side seams A–B. With right sides together, oversew the two pieces together between points A and C for the centre front and back seams. Press the seams flat.

TOY SOLDIER: Gather round the waist and the bottom of each leg, but do not draw up. Fit on doll. Draw up the gathers around the waist and legs, and secure.

HANSEL: Bind the top edge, then thread the elastic through and secure. Fit on doll. Draw the top edge up over his shirt so waist is under arms.

PRINCE FLORIMUND: Gather round the waist and bottom of each leg, but do not draw up. Fit on doll. Draw the top edge up well above the waist and secure the gathers close under the arms.

Draw up the leg gathers and glue black braid over them. Then make two butterfly bows from 12cm (4½in) lengths of black satin ribbon (see Basics 6). Mark points B 3.5cm (1⅜in) from point A. Stitch or glue to side of leg, over the braid.

SHOES, PUMPS, SLIPPERS

1. Cut the upper four times and the sole twice – either all in one colour or with contrast soles (see individual doll for patterns).
2. For each shoe, join two uppers, oversewing at the front and back. Pin the lower edge to the sole, matching seams to notches, then oversew. Turn to the right side.
3. See individual directions for trimming and so on.

CHAPTER 1

The Three Bears decide to go for a Picnic

Mrs Bear hummed a tune as she prepared the porridge. Her husband was having his bath, so she had wrapped Baby Bear in a big towel to keep him out of mischief.

'It's a lovely sunny morning,' she called to them both. 'Let's go for a walk in the woods after breakfast.'

'Could we take a picnic?' shrieked Baby Bear excitedly.

'Well, I suppose we *could*,' agreed Mother Bear thoughtfully. 'I've been baking this week, because Goldilocks is coming to stay, so there's plenty of food in the larder.' Goldilocks was Baby Bear's favourite cousin. 'But she's coming on the six o'clock bus, so we must be back before she gets here.'

'Right,' said Father Bear, getting out of the bath. 'Leave the porridge until we get home. We'll be off as soon as the picnic basket is ready.'

He sliced a loaf of crusty bread and helped Mother Bear to make thick honey sandwiches.

Then they packed them into the basket, together with a large pork pie, sausage rolls, plump red tomatoes, a bunch of radishes, some spicy currant buns, fruit cake, gingerbread, pumpkin pie and jam tarts, a large bag of shiny apples, a flask of tea, another of cold milk and a bottle of lemonade.

Baby Bear was struggling to pick up his big storybook. 'So that Daddy can read to me when I have my rest,' he explained. 'And if I don't have a rest,' he added threateningly, 'I get hiccups.'

'There's no more room,' said Mother Bear firmly, 'but don't worry; all your favourite fairytales are stored up in Father Bear's head.'

Baby Bear looked at his father's head and hoped it was big enough to hold *all* his favourite stories. But he decided Father Bear really did have a very big head, so perhaps they were all there.

Mother Bear tied on her Sunday-best hat and straightened Baby Bear's new sailor suit. Father Bear put on his warm woolly cap and scarf in case he caught a cold.

And they were ready to go.

Mother Bear

Choose a fairly firm, medium-weight cotton-type fabric for Mother Bear's dress and matching cape. The apron and mob cap are best made up in a lighter weight fabric, but if you have to use a similar weight to the dress, omit the interlining.

MATERIALS

50cm (⅝yd) medium-weight cotton-type fabric, 90cm (36in) wide, for dress and cape

Light-weight cotton-type fabric: 40cm (16in) diameter circle for the mob cap and 19 × 30cm (7½ × 12in), for apron

25 × 80cm (10 × 30in) medium-weight cotton-type fabric, for petticoat

10 × 20cm (4 × 8in) olive green felt, for hat

40cm (16in) diameter circle light-weight iron-on interlining for the mob cap (optional, see above)

3m (3¼yd) black lace, 15mm (⅝in) deep

1.3m (1½yd) white lace, 30mm (1¼in) deep, for cap

60cm (¾yd) white lace, 30mm (1¼in) deep, for hat

45cm (½yd) white lace, 15mm (⅝in) deep, for collar

80cm (1yd) narrow white lace 10mm (⅜in wide), for petticoat

50cm (½yd) Rosy Mauve (pink) Sheer Multi-stripe ribbon, 23mm (⅞in) wide, for cap

1.5m (1¾yd) Rosy Mauve (pink) Sheer Multi-stripe ribbon, 23mm (⅞in) wide, for hat

1.7m (2yd) Willow (green) Sheer Multi-stripe ribbon, 23mm (⅞in) wide, for hat

2.1m (2¼yd) Colonial Rose single-face satin ribbon, 16mm (⅝in) wide, for hat

50cm (½yd) black satin ribbon, 3mm (⅛in) wide, for cape ties

40cm (½yd) matching (or white) bias binding for neck

1.3m (1½yd) matching (or white) bias binding, for cap

2m (2¼yd) narrow round elastic

3 snap-fasteners

Matching threads

Stiff card for hat (cereal carton)

Dry stick adhesive (optional)

Clear adhesive

MOTHER BEAR'S LACE-TRIMMED PETTICOAT

1. Join the two short edges of the fabric for centre back seam. Turn under and stitch a 1cm (⅜in) hem around the top edge. Turn under and stitch a narrow hem around the lower edge. Sew lace on the right side to overlap the lower edge.

2. Thread 40cm (16in) elastic through waist hem and draw up to fit.

3. Make shoulder straps from 60cm (24in) elastic. Stitch centre of elastic to the top edge of the petticoat at centre front, then stitch the two ends at the centre back.

MOTHER BEAR'S ROSE-PINK DRESS AND SHOULDER CAPE

4. Cut a strip of fabric 26 × 90cm (10½ × 36in) for the skirt, and a strip 10 × 80cm (4 × 32in) for the cape. Cut bodice front and cape collar once each, the bodice back and sleeve twice each.

5. Join the bodice front to the back pieces at the shoulders. Gather round the top of each sleeve between the circles, then fit sleeves into armholes, matching the side edges and notches, and centre top to the shoulder seam. Draw up to fit, distributing the gathers evenly, and stitch into place. Clip the armhole curves. Join the sleeve seams and side seams of bodice.

6. Mark the top edge of the skirt into eight, then gather, beginning and ending 2cm (¾in) from each side edge. Pin the skirt to the lower edge of the bodice, matching the marked points to the side seams and notches. Draw up the gathers to fit and stitch into place. Join the centre back seam of the skirt, leaving 8cm (3in) open at the top.

7. Turn under the centre back edges of the bodice along the broken line and stitch. Bind the neck edge. Gather white lace for the collar and pin evenly round the neck over the binding. Draw up to fit, distributing the gathers evenly, and stitch into place. Stitch snap fasteners to back opening at neck, centre and waist.

8. Mark the lower edge of each sleeve as indicated by the broken line, then stitch black lace with the straight edge just above the line and the rest of the lace overlapping it. Turn the raw edge under, then fold under along the marked line and make a hem. Thread 22cm (8½in) elastic through each hem and draw up to fit wrist.

9. Fit dress on bear to determine the length. Turn up the hem and stitch, then trim with black lace over stitching line.

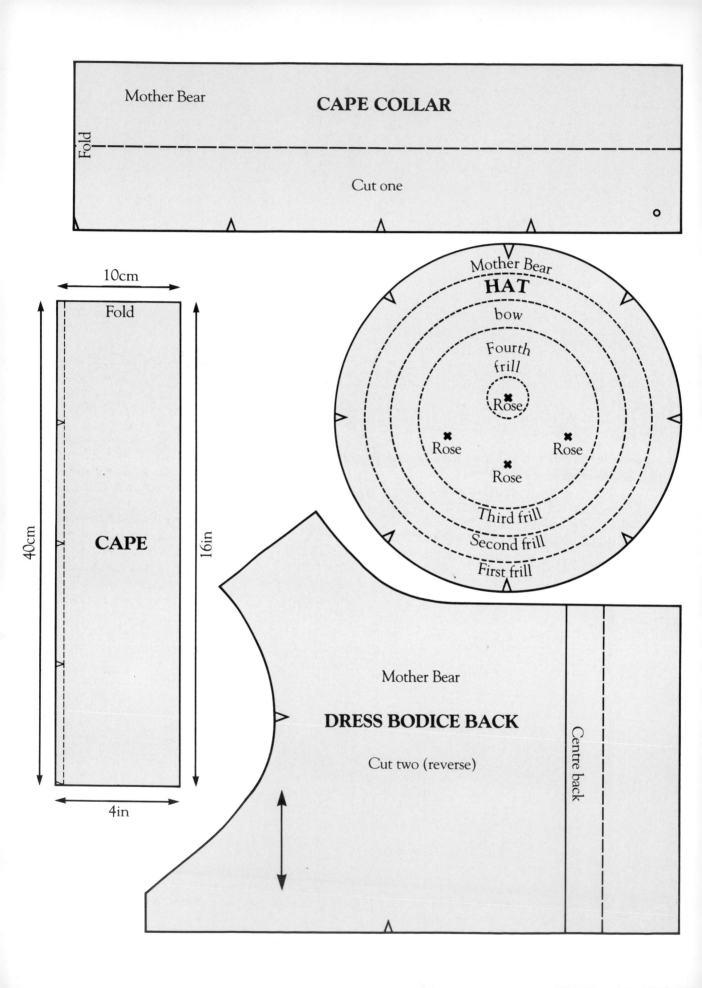

Mother Bear

CAPE COLLAR

Fold

Cut one

10cm

Fold

40cm

16in

CAPE

4in

Mother Bear

HAT

bow

Fourth frill

Rose

Rose Rose Rose

Third frill

Second frill

First frill

Mother Bear

DRESS BODICE BACK

Cut two (reverse)

Centre back

10. Make a very narrow hem along the lower edge of the cape and along the two short sides, to form centre front edges. Stitch black lace to overlap these edges, turning the corners neatly.

11. Mark the top edge into eight, then gather. With right sides together and raw edges matching, pin the top edge of the cape to the lower edge of the collar between the circles, matching the marked points to notches. Draw up the gathers to fit, distributing them evenly, and stitch.

12. With right side inside, fold the collar in half along the broken line, then join each short side end. Turn to the right side. Turn under the raw lower edge of the collar and stitch neatly over gathers on inside of cape.

13. Stitch lace around collar, turning the cut ends over each end and finishing neatly on the inside. Cut the black ribbon in half and stitch inside front edges of collar to form ties.

MOTHER BEAR'S DAISY-PATTERN APRON AND MATCHING MOB CAP

14. Make a very narrow hem along the side and lower edges of the apron fabric. Mark the top edge into eight, then gather. Mark the lower edge of the bodice front 4cm (1½in) from each side seam, then divide the area between these two marks into eight. With right sides together, position the apron upside down over the bodice, so that the raw top edge of the apron is level with the waist seam of the dress. Pin together, matching the marked points. Draw up the gathers to fit and stitch neatly, then turn the apron down to fall over the skirt.

15. If you are using interlining for the mob cap, cut a 40cm (16in) diameter circle and press onto the wrong side of the fabric, following the instructions, then cut fabric level. Stitch binding all round the edge, turning the whole width of the binding over to the inside and stitching neatly to form a channel. Stitch the straight edge of the lace to the very edge of the circle so that it overlaps beyond (don't try to make it lie flat). Thread 50cm (20in) elastic through the channel and draw up to fit the head.

16. For the bow, glue two 23cm (9in) lengths of pink Multi-stripe ribbon together by overlapping the side edges a fraction, then make a formal bow (see Basics 6). Stitch at centre front of cap.

MOTHER BEAR'S SUNDAY-BEST HAT

17. Cut a circle of thin card as shown in the pattern. Using stick adhesive, glue to felt (or use clear adhesive, but use it sparingly or it will impede your needle when you sew). Cut felt 2-3mm (⅛in) beyond edge of card. Glue other side of card to felt, then cut level with the first side. Oversew edges of felt together.

18. Glue cut ends of white lace to form a circle, then mark into eight and gather. Mark outer edge of felt circle with pins as notches. Matching marked points, pin the gathered edge just underneath the edge of the circle so that the lace overlaps beyond. Draw up gathers to fit and stitch.

19. Glue cut ends of a 60cm (25in) length of green Multi-stripe ribbon to form a circle, then mark into eight and gather one long edge. Pin the gathered edge to the top of circle 10mm (⅜in) from the edge (first frill on the pattern), following the notches as before.

20. Prepare a 50cm (21in) length of green ribbon as step 19. Stitch to the hat about 7mm (¼in) inside previous frill (second frill on the pattern).

21. Repeat step 20 with a 40cm (17in) length of green ribbon (third frill on the pattern).

22. Make a formal bow (see Basics 6) from 15cm (6in) pink Multi-stripe ribbon, but do not bind the centre with ribbon. Glue two 17.5cm (7in) lengths of ribbon together by overlapping the side edges a fraction and make another bow. Glue three 20cm (8in) lengths of ribbon together in the same way and make a third bow. Place the second bow on top of the third bow, with centres matching, then place the first bow on top of the second. Push your needle through the centre of all three bows, then bind securely together. Stitch to the hat at centre back of area inside the frills, as indicated.

23. Glue cut ends of a 20cm (8in) length of green ribbon to form a circle, then gather and draw up to make a rosette with a 10mm (⅜in) hole in the centre. Stitch immediately in front of triple-bow (see pattern), so that the frill overlaps the bound centre of the bow.

24. Make four roses (see Basics 6) using 30cm (12in) Colonial Rose satin ribbon for each. Glue one rose in the centre of the ribbon rosette, then glue the other three in front (at the points marked with an X on the pattern).

25. Fold a 40cm (16in) length of pink Multi-stripe ribbon in half and stitch under back of the hat to form streamers. Trim cut ends into an inverted V-shape.

26. Use remaining satin ribbon to make ties. Stitch centre of ribbon underneath hat so that the ends extend at each side. Tie in a bow under her chin.

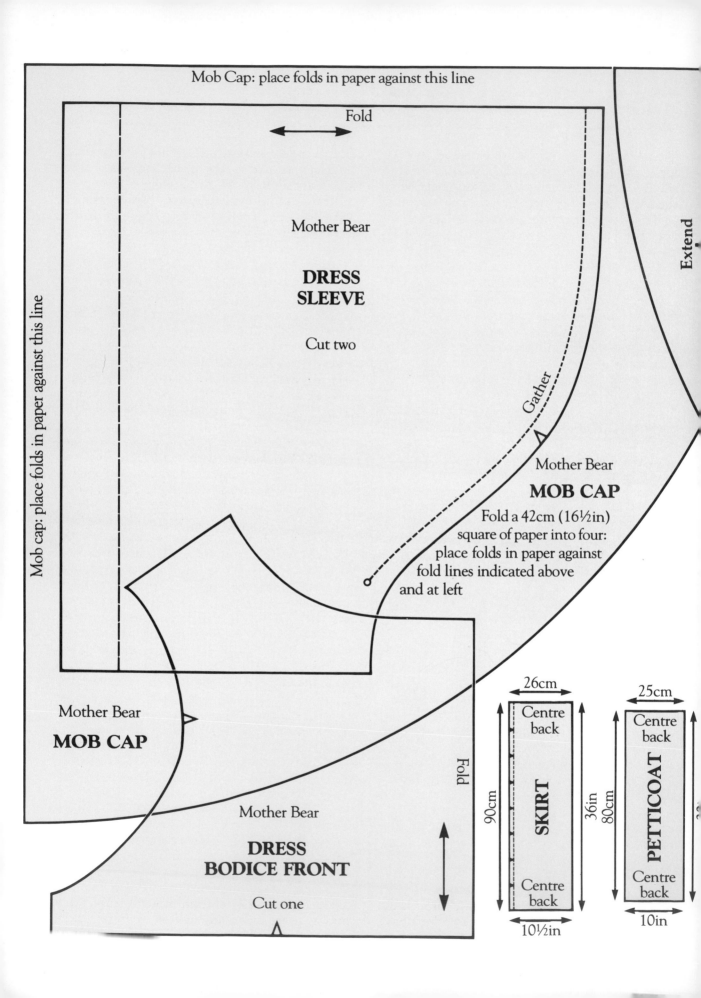

Mob Cap: place folds in paper against this line

Fold

Mother Bear

DRESS SLEEVE

Cut two

Mob cap: place folds in paper against this line

Extend

Gather

Mother Bear

MOB CAP

Fold a 42cm (16½in) square of paper into four: place folds in paper against fold lines indicated above and at left

Mother Bear

MOB CAP

Mother Bear

DRESS BODICE FRONT

Cut one

Fold

26cm

Centre back

SKIRT

90cm

36in

Centre back

10½in

25cm

Centre back

PETTICOAT

80cm

Centre back

10in

Goldilocks

Crisp broderie anglaise makes a very special pinafore, but any pretty fabric will do – just cut it to size, allowing a little extra to make a hem along the lower edge. Look for a light-weight dress fabric patterned with tiny flowers, then match it with ribbon for the satin roses to trim Goldilocks' demure bonnet.

MATERIALS

50cm (½yd) light-weight printed cotton-type dress fabric, 90cm (36in) wide

20cm (8in) white cotton-type fabric, 50cm (20in) wide, for pantalettes

50cm (½yd) broderie anglaise (eyelet embroidery), 14cm (5½in) deep, for pinafore

35cm (14in) broderie anglaise (eyelet embroidery), 35mm (1⅜in) deep, for straps

30cm (12in) bias binding, to match dress

45cm (½yd) white bias binding, for pinafore

75cm (⅞yd) black lace, 10mm (⅜in) deep, to trim dress

1m (1¼yd) lace, 10mm (⅜in) deep, to trim pantalettes

2m (2¼yd) single-face satin ribbon, 10mm (⅜in) wide, to tone with fabric

50cm (20in) narrow braid, to edge bonnet brim

1m (1yd) narrow round elastic

4 snap-fasteners

Matching threads

20 × 30cm (8 × 12in) thin card, for bonnet (or Vilene – see step 8)

Dry-stick adhesive (if using card)

Clear adhesive

GOLDILOCKS' LACE-EDGED PANTALETTES

1. Cut the pattern piece twice in fabric.
2. Fold each piece in half and join the side seam between points A–B. With right sides together, join the two pieces between points A–C for the centre front and back seams. Clip the curve and press the seams open.
3. Turn under the raw top edge and make a 1cm (⅜in) hem. Turn up a narrow hem around the lower edge of each leg. Turn to the right side.
4. Thread 30cm (12in) round elastic through the waist hem and draw up to fit. (As bears don't have very well-defined waistlines, you can save Goldilocks any embarrassment by adding elastic straps as for Mother Bear's petticoat (step 3)).
5. Trim each leg with two rows of lace, the first just overlapping the lower edge and the second just overlapping the first.

GOLDILOCKS' FLOWERY DRESS AND VICTORIAN BONNET

6. If you are using a fine fabric cut a strip of fabric 15 × 90cm (6 × 36in) for the skirt. If you are using a medium-weight fabric, cut the skirt about 60cm (24in) wide. Before you cut the bodice and sleeves, check that you will have a sufficient area of fabric for the bonnet (see step 8), then cut the bodice front once and the bodice back and sleeve twice each.
7. Follow the directions for Mother Bear's dress (steps 5–9 inclusive), with the following exceptions. *Step 6*: Leave only 6cm (2½in) open at the top of the centre back seam. *Step 7*: Stitch black lace flat over the neck binding, the straight edge of the lace being level with the lower edge of the binding to form a tiny stand-up collar. *Step 8*: Thread only 15cm (6in) elastic through each wrist hem. *Step 9*: Omit lace trim on hem.
8. (*Note*: For a softer, washable bonnet, use heavy Vilene instead of card, and stitch the fabric to it, instead of gluing.) Cut bonnet brim in thin card (ignore the broken lines). Using dry-stick adhesive, glue one side (the top) to wrong side of fabric. Cut level with card all round. Cover underside with fabric in the same way. Cut outer edge level again, but leave a 2cm (¾in) overlap along the inner curved edge (as indicated by the broken lines). Snip overlap into 1cm (⅜in) wide tabs, as indicated.
9. Cut a strip of card 2 × 24cm (¾ × 9½in). Cover the underside with fabric and trim level all round. With the uncovered side uppermost, fit strip round inner curve of brim, edges absolutely level, and hold together by gluing the tabs, one by one, under the fabric-covered strip. Trim the ends of the strip level with the side edges of the brim.
10. Cut the bonnet back twice in fabric. Stitch together along the bottom straight edge, then turn to right side and tack all round, making

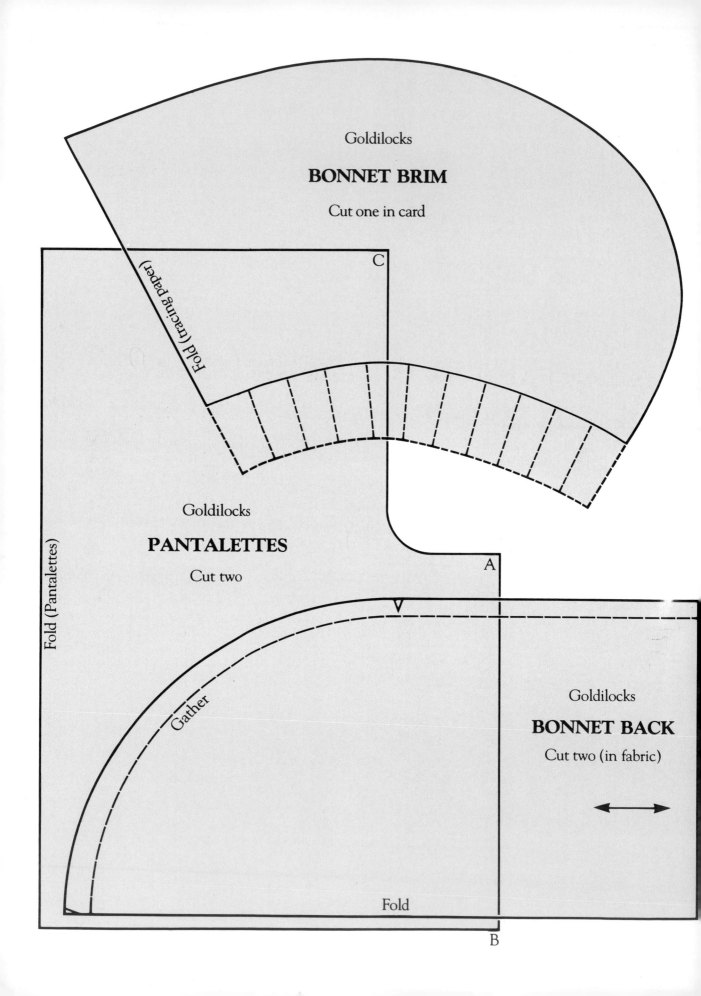

Goldilocks

BONNET BRIM

Cut one in card

C

Fold (tracing paper)

Goldilocks

PANTALETTES

Cut two

A

V

Fold (Pantalettes)

Gather

Goldilocks

BONNET BACK

Cut two (in fabric)

Fold

B

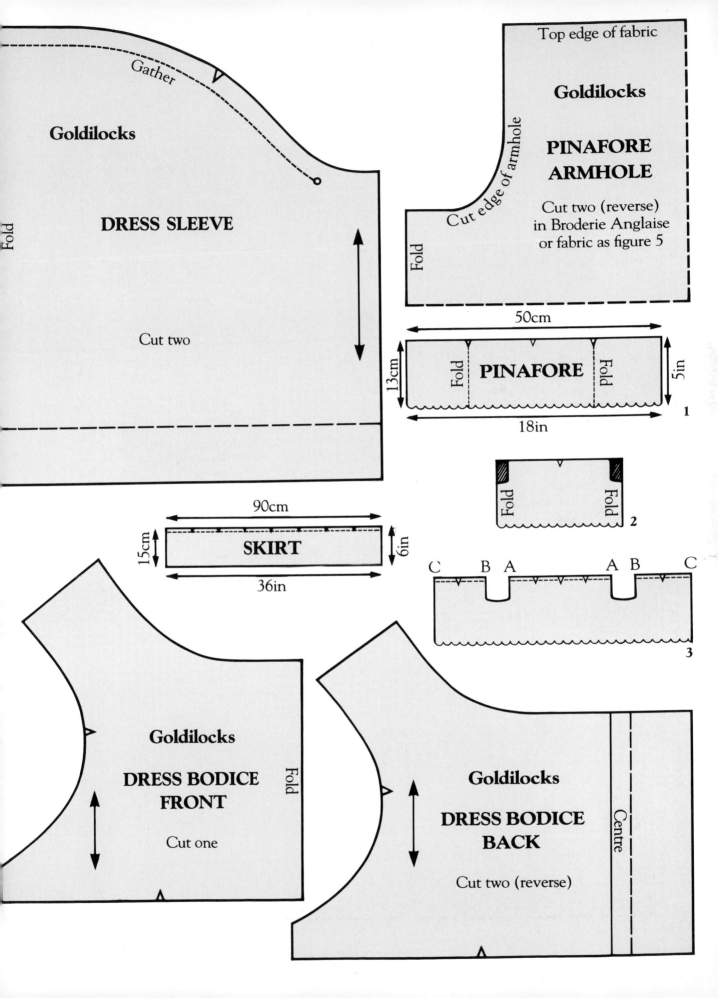

Goldilocks

DRESS SLEEVE

Cut two

Gather

Fold

Goldilocks

PINAFORE ARMHOLE

Cut two (reverse)
in Broderie Anglaise
or fabric as figure 5

Top edge of fabric

Cut edge of armhole

Fold

50cm

13cm

Fold **PINAFORE** Fold

5in

18in

1

Fold   Fold

2

90cm

15cm **SKIRT** 6in

36in

C   B A   A B   C

3

Goldilocks

DRESS BODICE FRONT

Cut one

Fold

Goldilocks

DRESS BODICE BACK

Cut two (reverse)

Centre

sure that the cut edges are absolutely level. Press. Mark the centre top and notches, then gather all round, beginning and ending at the lower corners. Mark the uncovered top of the card strip equally into four, then pin gathers over back edge, lower corners of back at each end of the strip, and the centre top and notches matching the marked points. Draw up to fit, then glue into position, distributing gathers evenly between the pins.

11. Cut another 2 × 24cm (¾ × 9½in) strip of card. Measure it over the previous strip (allowing for the gathered fabric) and trim off any excess. Cut a strip of fabric 5 × 27cm (2 × 10¾in) and glue the card strip to the wrong side, the fabric overlapping equally all round. Fold the surplus fabric over the long side edges and glue smoothly to underside of card: glue this strip over top of previous strip to cover gathers. Fold under any surplus at each end and glue neatly inside the bonnet.

12. Gather along the straight back edge. Fit bonnet on bear and draw up gathers to fit across the back of head so that the brim is drawn back to frame the face.

13. Make five ribbon roses (see Basics 6), using 25–30cm (10–12in) for each. Glue one rose at the centre top of the covered strip, over the angle between the strip and brim. Glue two more roses close together at each side.

14. Cut the remaining ribbon in half and stitch one piece inside the bonnet at each end of strip, to form ties. Make a bow under Goldilocks' chin and trim the ribbon in an inverted V-shape.

GOLDILOCKS' FRILLY BRODERIE ANGLAISE PINAFORE

15. Cut broderie anglaise 13cm (5in) deep × 50cm (18in) wide. If using fabric instead, add sufficient to depth to make a narrow hem. Turn under a narrow hem down each side edge. Mark top edge into four (figure 1), then fold along broken lines.

16. To cut each armhole, place the pattern level with the top edge and the fold line, as figure 2. Bind the armhole edges.

17. Mark the top edge of the front (points A–A on figure 3) into four, then gather and draw up to measure 10cm (4in). Bind the raw edge, distributing the gathers evenly. Gather and bind the two back top edges (points C–B and B–C) in the same way, drawing up each to 5cm (2in).

18. For each shoulder strap, cut a 9cm (3½in) length of bias binding, fold it in half lengthways and neatly oversew the edges together. Stitch ends behind top corners of front and back (points A–B), with folded edge towards centre of pinafore.

19. Cut a 16cm (6½in) length of narrow broderie anglaise. Mark the top edge into eight, then turn the long raw edge under and gather very close to the fold. Mark the strap into eight, then pin the broderie anglaise on top, level with the inner edge and matching the marked points. Draw up gathers to fit and stitch. Turn under and gather the cut ends neatly around the top corners of pinafore.

20. Stitch a snap-fastener at the top of centre back opening.

Father Bear

Any firm fabric would be suitable for Father Bear's trousers. And although there is an indication of the yarn and size of needles, which were used to make the knitted garments, measurements are also given, so you can use any left-over balls of yarn.

MATERIALS

25cm (10in) fine needlecord 60cm (24in) wide
35cm (14in) check gingham, 60cm (24in) wide, for shirt
50cm (20in) elastic, 2cm (¾in) wide, for braces
40cm (16in) white bias binding (or to tone with colour of shirt fabric)
20cm (8in) single-face satin ribbon, 23mm (⅞in) wide, for bow-tie
3 snap-fasteners
Matching threads
Yarn and knitting needles for hat and scarf (see below)
Thin card

FATHER BEAR'S CHECK SHIRT AND BOW-TIE

1. Cut the back once, and the front and sleeve twice each, in gingham.

2. Join the front pieces to the back at the shoulders. Gather round the top of each sleeve

between the circles, then fit sleeves into armholes, matching side edges and notches, and centre top to the shoulder seam. Draw up to fit, distributing gathers evenly, and stitch into place. Clip armhole curves. Join sleeve and side seams.

3. Turn under and stitch a very narrow hem around the lower edge of each sleeve, and down each front edge. Make a 1cm (⅜in) hem around the lower edge. Turn under and stitch front edges as broken line. Turn up and stitch sleeve hems.

4. Bind neckline neatly, folding binding over raw edge.

5. Stitch snap-fasteners at neck, centre and waist (at points marked O).

6. Make a formal bow (see Basics 6) for the bow-tie, using 14cm (5½in) ribbon for the bow, and 4cm (1½in) to bind centre. Stitch over the top snap-fastener.

FATHER BEAR'S TROUSERS

7. Cut the pattern piece twice in fabric.

8. Fold each piece in half and join the side seams between points A–B. Right sides together, join the two pieces between A–C for centre front and back seams. Clip curve and press seams open.

9. Turn under the raw top edge and make a 1cm (⅜in) hem. Turn up a narrow hem around the lower edge of each leg. Turn to right side.

10. Cut elastic in half. Stitch one end of each piece inside the front waist edge at X on each side. Fit trousers on bear. Bring both pieces over his shoulders and pin ends (at an angle) inside centre back of waist, one crossing over the other. Check length is correct. Before removing trousers, turn up leg hems and pin.

11. Sew straps into place and stitch leg hems.

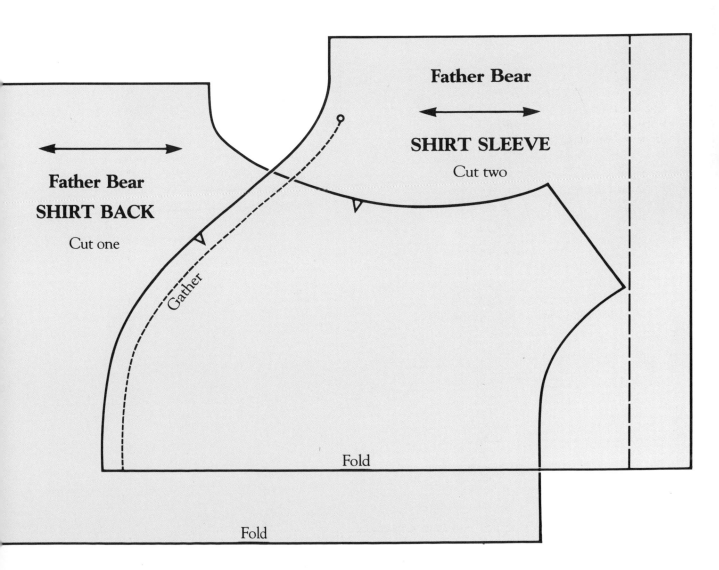

Father Bear
SHIRT BACK
Cut one

Gather

Fold

Father Bear
SHIRT SLEEVE
Cut two

Fold

FATHER BEAR'S KNITTED HAT AND SCARF

Apart from very thin or very thick yarns, you can use almost any weight for Father Bear's woolly hat and scarf. Details of the yarn and needles that were used are given only as an indication. All you have to do is to knit each piece to the correct size. Knit a small sample piece with your yarn, using needles of an appropriate size to suit the thickness. Measure how many stitches and how many rows, to 2cm (or 1in), and then work out the number of stitches and rows you will need to knit pieces to the sizes indicated.

Note: Two 50g (2oz) balls of double-knit wool, one in each colour, made the hat and scarf illustrated. To achieve a tension of five stitches and approximately six rows to 2cm (or six stitches and approximately eight rows to 1in), a pair of 3¾mm (No 9) needles were used.

HAT

Cast on a sufficient number of stitches in blue yarn to make a piece about 46cm (18in) wide. You must choose a number which is divisible by eight. (*Note*: Using double knit wool and No 9 needles, 120 stitches were needed.)

Work 8–10 rows (about 3cm/1¼in) in knit 1, purl 1 rib.
Next row: knit.
Next row: purl.
Repeat these two rows until the work measures 13cm (5in), ending with a purl row.
Next row: knit 2 together. Repeat to end of row.
Next row: purl.
Repeat these two rows twice more.
Break off the yarn, leaving a short length, and thread it through the remaining stitches. Draw up tightly and stitch securely, then join the two side edges to form the centre back seam of the hat.
In contrast yarn, cast on a sufficient number of stitches to make a piece 5cm (2in) wide. (*Note*: Using double knit wool and No 9 needles, 12 stitches were needed.)
First row: knit.
Repeat this row until the band is long enough to fit loosely round the bear's head (about 44cm/17in). Cast off.
Join the two short ends to form the centre back seam, then pin band evenly round hat, over ribbing, right side of band to wrong side of hat, lower edges level. Oversew together. Turn hat to the right side and turn band up over ribbing, just below the stitching line. Catch band to hat at centre back and front and sides, to hold in place.

Use contrast yarn to make the pompon. Cut two 6cm (2¼in) circles of card with a 2cm (¾in) hole in the centre, as pattern. Fold a 4m (4yd) length of yarn into four and thread into a tapestry needle (have fewer strands if yarn is thicker). Wrap the yarn evenly over and over the two card circles (as figure 4), continuing until the central hole is full (figure 5).

Push pointed scissors through the yarn and between the two card circles (see arrow on figure 5). Cut yarn all round (keeping scissors between the card). Slip a 30cm (12in) length of double yarn between the two layers of card to surround yarn in centre. Knot together, pulling as tight as you can. Cut away the card, then trim pompon severely (but not the ties) to make a neat, round, firm ball.

With your tapestry needle, thread ties through centre top of hat: pull tight inside and stitch securely.

SCARF

Cast on a sufficient number of stitches in blue yarn to make a piece 10cm (4in) wide. (*Note*: Using double knit wool and No 9 needles, 24 stitches were needed.)
First row: knit.
Repeat this row until the work measures 2.5cm (1in), then change to mauve yarn. Work the same number of rows to make a contrast stripe, twisting the two threads together at the end of every second row, so that the spare yarn is carried tidily up the side of the work.

Change back to blue yarn and continue in this way, making alternate stripes, until the work measures 60cm (24in), ending with a mauve stripe. Cast off.

Make a knotted fringe along each end of the scarf with contrast yarn. Cut thirteen 12cm (5in) lengths of yarn in each colour. Cut each length in half. Put the two lengths together and fold in half. Push folded end through scarf between two stitches just above the cast-on (or cast-off) edge, then draw the four cut ends through the loop and pull taut. Make a knot at each corner, with the remaining eleven between.

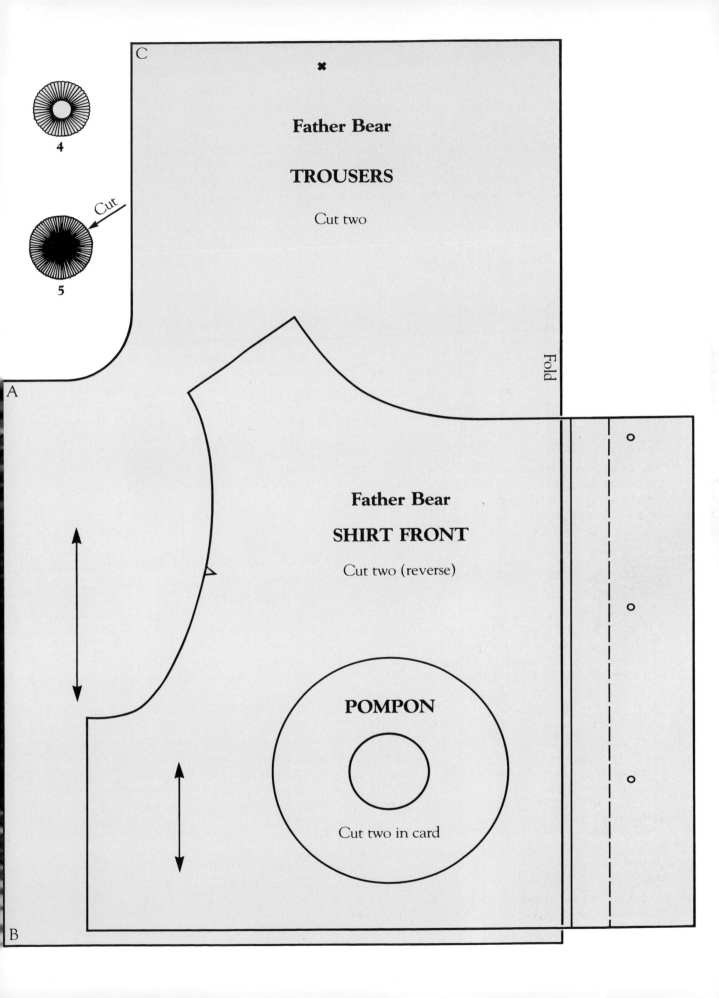

C

Father Bear

TROUSERS

Cut two

4

Cut

5

A

Father Bear

SHIRT FRONT

Cut two (reverse)

Fold

POMPON

Cut two in card

B

Baby Bear

If you can't find any striped fabric for Baby Bear's dickey, use plain white, and bind the top edge with blue binding, or use blue felt, and add a stripe of white braid to match the tunic. If you don't want to edge the hat brim with braid, cut the felt a fraction away from the edge of the card, then oversew the edges neatly together.

MATERIALS

35cm (14in) blue felt, 90cm (36in) wide
Blue and white horizontally striped fabric, 7cm (3in) deep × 14cm (5½in) wide
1m (1yd) white Russian braid
70cm (¾yd) black double-face satin ribbon, 10mm (⅜in) wide
50cm (20in) narrow blue braid, to edge hat
25cm (10in) narrow black elastic
4 snap-fasteners
Matching threads
Stiff card (cereal carton)
Dry-stick adhesive (optional)
Clear adhesive

BABY BEAR'S SAILOR TUNIC

1. In blue felt, cut the back and collar once each, and the front and sleeve twice each.
2. Stitch Russian braid close to outer edges of collar and sleeves, as broken lines.
3. Oversew front pieces to the back at shoulders. Pin right side of collar to wrong side of tunic, between single notches, matching centre back points and triple notches at each side. Oversew

together. Fold centre front edges under, as broken line, and stitch.
4. Gather round the top of each sleeve, between circles, then pin sleeves into armholes, matching side edges, and centre top to shoulder seam. Draw up gathers to fit and stitch sleeves into place. Join sleeve and side seams. Turn to right side.
5. Fit tunic on bear and overlap front edges. Mark position for two snap-fasteners and sew into place.
6. If possible, use the selvedge for the top edge of the insertion; otherwise, cut a little deeper and make a hem along the top. Turn under a narrow hem around the side and lower edges. Stitch one half of a snap-fastener inside each tunic front at point O. Place insertion flat on the bear's chest, then close the tunic over it and mark position of fasteners on fabric so they fall close to top edge. Sew remaining halves of fasteners to the insertion.
7. Make a 14cm (5½in) length of ribbon into a butterfly bow (see Basics 6). Mark points B 4cm (1½in) from A. Stitch at centre front of tunic, immediately below the collar.

BABY BEAR'S SAILOR HAT

8. For the brim, cut a 15cm (6in) diameter circle of stiff card (double thickness cereal carton) with a 9cm (3½in) hole in the centre; as shown in the pattern (ignore the broken lines). Using glue stick (or thinly spread adhesive) cover one side of the card smoothly with felt. Cut felt level with the inner and outer edges (this is the top). Cover the underside in the same way, but cut the central hole only 6cm (2¼in) diameter and cut this overlap into tabs (see broken lines).
9. Cut a 3 × 30cm (1¼ × 12in) strip of card (single thickness cereal carton) for side of crown (see diagram). Place this flat on your felt and draw round it. Remove card and cut felt along the marked line. Keep this piece for later use. Curve the card strip into a circle and fit inside centre of brim, allowing it to open out to fit snugly. Mark overlap, then remove and glue join. Fit back inside the brim, then carefully glue the tabs up inside to hold it in place.
10. Cut a 9cm (3½in) circle of (double-thickness) card for the top of the crown, and a 12cm (4½in) circle of felt, as pattern. Glue card in centre of felt, then cut V-shaped notches

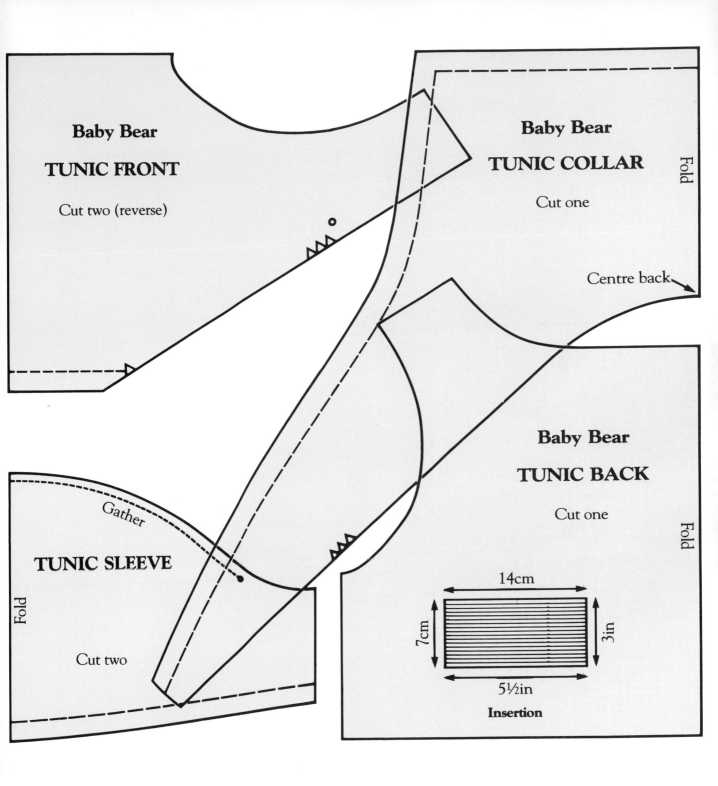

Baby Bear

TUNIC FRONT

Cut two (reverse)

Baby Bear

TUNIC COLLAR

Cut one

Fold

Centre back

TUNIC SLEEVE

Gather

Fold

Cut two

Baby Bear

TUNIC BACK

Cut one

Fold

14cm

7cm

3in

5½in

Insertion

all round the surplus, to form tiny tabs (as broken lines). Spread glue on the underside of four tabs (see points marked X). Place crown, card side down, on top of side strip, and press tabs down to hold it in position, then glue remaining tabs down.
11. Glue the previously cut strip of felt smoothly around the side, overlap at back. Cut another strip of single card, 2.5 × 30cm (1 × 2in), and glue it inside the hat to neaten.
12. Glue braid round edge of brim (or oversew).
13. Fold a 20cm (8in) length of ribbon in half (at a slight angle). Stitch the fold at centre back between brim and crown to hang down over brim, then glue ribbon round crown.
14. Stitch knotted ends of elastic just inside hat, at each side, to fit under chin.

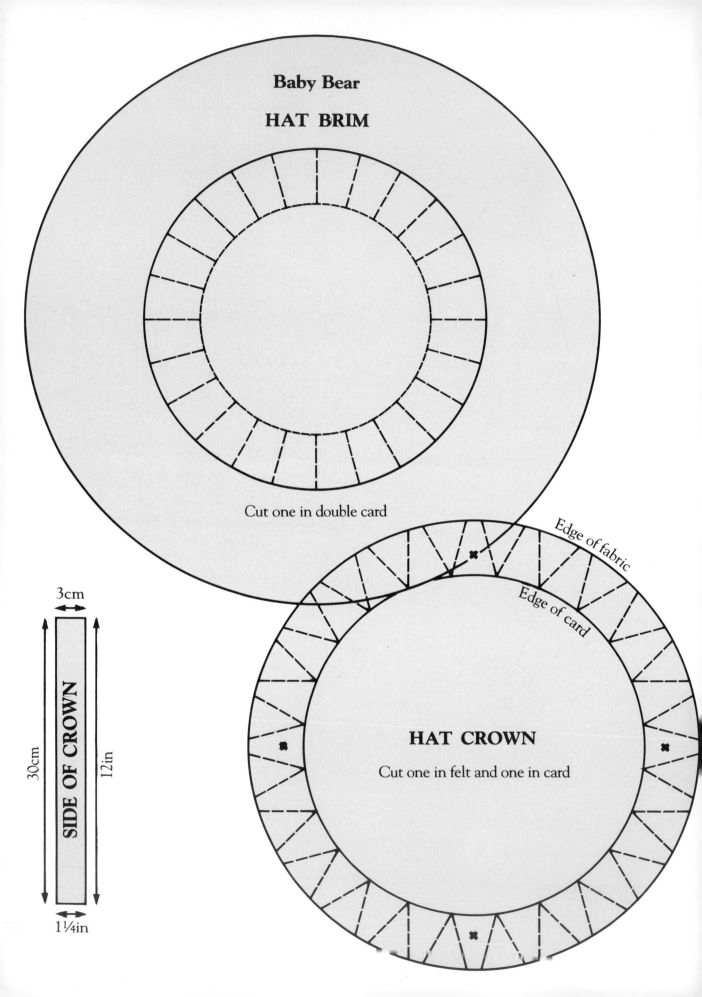

Baby Bear

HAT BRIM

Cut one in double card

Edge of fabric

Edge of card

HAT CROWN

Cut one in felt and one in card

3cm

30cm

12in

SIDE OF CROWN

1¼in

CHAPTER 2

The Mad Hatter's Tea-Party

Baby Bear loved the woods. He could imagine mysteries and adventures behind every tree. He walked on tip-toe not to make a noise. But walking on tip-toe isn't easy for bears and it made him tired. The Three Bears sat down to rest on a grassy bank and Mother Bear poured Baby Bear a mug of milk. Baby Bear wanted an adventure story while they were eating their shiny currant buns, so Father Bear suggested *Alice's Adventures in Wonderland*.

Baby Bear loved hearing the strange things that happened to a little girl who fell down a rabbit hole. His favourite part was when Alice found the Mad Hatter and the March Hare having a tea-party, with a dormouse asleep in the teapot.

Just then an enormous brown butterfly landed on Baby Bear's nose, making him sneeze. He jumped up and chased it as it fluttered off into the trees.

Mother Bear hurried after him, calling a warning to be careful of rabbit holes. Father Bear followed behind, grumbling about badly behaved baby bears.

Suddenly, they saw a table set for tea, with Alice, the Mad Hatter and the March Hare, and the dormouse, in the teapot.

Alice welcomed them with a big smile. The Hatter grinned broadly and the March Hare nodded happily as he continued pushing the sleepy dormouse into the teapot.

Baby Bear could hardly believe that Alice was holding his paw and telling him what a crazy tea-party it was. She said that they kept asking her stupid riddles, and even when she thought she knew the answer, they told her she was wrong.

Nobody offered the bears a cup of tea. Not that they really fancied any – with a dormouse in the teapot! It was all very confusing. Then Baby Bear saw the butterfly again. He ran after it; followed by his mother and father.

Back on the grassy bank, Baby Bear shouted, 'We've been to Wonderland!'

'These woods are magic,' his mother explained calmly, 'and that's a magic butterfly. Now stop getting over-excited and wipe your sticky paws.'

And they set off again along the path.

Alice

If you look at the original Tenniel illustrations for Lewis Carroll's *Alice's Adventures in Wonderland*, you will notice that one of the things which makes Alice's dress so attractive is the very full tucked skirt. This pattern re-creates that effect, using a fairly light-weight fabric. But don't worry if your fabric is a little thicker than the recommended weight: just reduce the width of the skirt, so that there are not so many gathers around the waist.

It is also interesting to compare the Alice in Wonderland illustrations with those for *Through the Looking Glass*, which was published seven years later. At first glance, Alice looks just the same, but if you study the drawings carefully, you will see that her pinafore is much prettier in the second book, with a deep frill around the apron (echoed by lace in our design). She now wears very smart striped stockings and, holding back her long hair, the famous Alice-band appears for the first time.

So there's just a little of the future Alice in this representation of the Mad Hatter's tea-party.

MATERIALS

Three 30cm (12in) squares flesh-coloured felt

50g (2oz) ball mid-brown double-knit yarn, for hair

For other materials, see Basics 8, items 1–9 inclusive

40cm (½yd) light-weight mid-blue cotton-type fabric, 90 or 115cm (36 or 45in) wide, for dress

18 × 35cm (7 × 14in) medium-weight white cotton-type fabric, for pinafore

50cm (⅝yd) light-weight white cotton-type fabric, 90cm (36in) wide, for petticoat and pantalettes

12 × 20cm (4½ × 8in) black felt, for shoes

or 10 × 15cm (4 × 6in) black (or coloured) felt for the uppers and a 10cm (4in) square of brown for the soles

1.1m (1¼yd) white lace, 20mm (¾in) deep, for pinafore

45cm (½yd) single-face blue satin ribbon to match dress, 23mm (⅞in) wide, for hairband

1.2m (1⅜yd) white grosgrain ribbon, 23mm (⅞in) wide, for pinafore

20cm (8in) double-face black satin ribbon, 3mm (⅛in) wide, for shoes

15cm (6in) pale blue bias binding

1m (1¼yd) narrow round elastic

3 snap-fasteners

Matching threads

ALICE: THE BASIC FIGURE

Follow the directions for the basic Fairytale Doll on page 19, using blue sequins for the eyes. For an attractive variation, give Alice black stockings, by cutting the legs and soles in black felt. For Alice's hair see Basics 9.

ALICE'S PETTICOAT AND PANTALETTES

1. Cut a 25cm (10in) deep strip right across the width of the fabric for the petticoat.
2. Join the two side edges to form the centre back seam. Turn under the raw top edge and then make a 1cm (⅜in) hem.
3. Make a similar hem, 1.5cm (⅝in) deep, around the lower edge. Now fold the fabric, on the right side, 2.5cm (1in) above the lower edge. Pin or tack to hold it in place, then stitch 5mm (¼in) from the folded edge to make a narrow tuck just above the hem. Tack down to hold in place before pressing.
4. Thread elastic through the top hem and draw up to fit the waist.
5. Follow the directions in Basics 10 to make Alice's pantalettes.

ALICE'S BLUE DRESS WITH TUCKED HEMLINE

6. Cut a strip 27cm (10½in) deep, right across the width of the fabric, for the skirt (see diagram). Then cut the bodice front once, and the back and sleeve twice each.
7. Join bodice front to back pieces at shoulders.
8. Mark the centre at the top edge of the sleeve, then gather between the circles. Fit the sleeve into the armhole of the bodice, matching the side edges and notches, and the centre top with the shoulder seam. Draw up the gathers to fit, distributing them evenly between the marked points, and stitch. Clip curves. When both sleeves are in place, join the side seams of the sleeves and bodice.
9. Mark the top edge of the skirt equally into eight, then gather, beginning and ending 2cm (¾in) from the side edges (see diagram). Pin to the lower edge of the bodice, side edges level, matching the marked points to the notches and

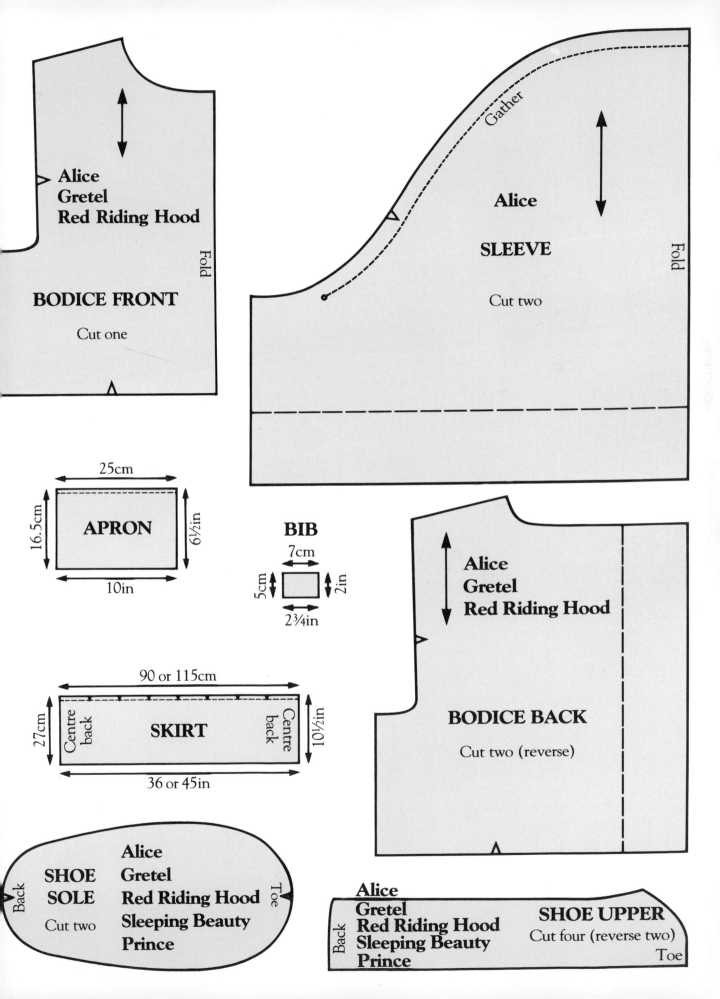

Alice
Gretel
Red Riding Hood

BODICE FRONT

Cut one

Fold

Alice

SLEEVE

Cut two

Gather

Fold

25cm

16.5cm

APRON

6½in

10in

BIB

7cm

5cm

2in

2¾in

90 or 115cm

27cm

Centre back

SKIRT

Centre back

10½in

36 or 45in

Alice
Gretel
Red Riding Hood

BODICE BACK

Cut two (reverse)

Back

SHOE
SOLE

Cut two

Alice
Gretel
Red Riding Hood
Sleeping Beauty
Prince

Toe

Alice
Gretel
Red Riding Hood
Sleeping Beauty
Prince

Back

SHOE UPPER
Cut four (reverse two)

Toe

seams. Draw up to fit, then stitch, distributing the gathers evenly. Turn seam up behind bodice. Join the centre back seam of the skirt, leaving 8cm (3in) open at the top. Turn under the centre back edges of the bodice as indicated by the broken line and stitch. Turn under and stitch the edges of the skirt opening to correspond (either stitch or leave free).

10. Bind the neck edge neatly.

11. Stitch snap-fasteners to the back opening at neck, centre and waist.

12. Turn under the raw lower edge of each sleeve, then fold under along the broken line and stitch the hem. Now make a second line of stitches, 5mm (¼in) below the first, to form a narrow channel. Thread elastic through and draw up to fit the arms.

13. Turn up and stitch a 2.5cm (1in) hem around the skirt. Fold the fabric 5.5cm (2⅛in) above the lower edge and make a 5mm (¼in) tuck as directed for the petticoat (step 3). Then fold the fabric 3.5cm (1⅜in) above the lower edge and make another tuck just below the first one. Tack and press as for the petticoat.

ALICE'S LACE-EDGED PINAFORE

14. Cut a piece of fabric 16.5cm (6½in) deep × 25cm (10in) wide for the skirt, and a piece 5cm (2in) deep × 7cm (2¾in) wide for the bib (see diagram).

15. Turn under and stitch a very narrow hem around the sides and lower edge of the skirt, then stitch lace on top, overlapping the edge of the fabric as illustrated. Gather neatly at each corner so that the lace lies flat.

16. Gather the top edge of the fabric (excluding lace) and draw up to measure 9cm (3½in). Cut an 80cm (⅞in) length of white ribbon for the waistband and ties. Matching the centre of the fabric to the centre of the ribbon, fold the ribbon in half lengthways over the top edge of the apron and stitch to form the waistband, distributing the gathers evenly between the edges of the ribbon. Continue stitching the edges of the folded ribbon together for another 4.5cm (1¾in) beyond the edge of the fabric at each side.

17. Fold a 7cm (2¾in) length of ribbon in half lengthways over the top edge of the bib to form a binding, and stitch neatly. Then bind each side edge in the same way, but with a 14cm (5½in) length of ribbon, having the cut edge of the ribbon level with the lower edge of the bib at each side and the remainder extending above the top edge. Continue to fold this extra ribbon in half lengthways and stitch the edges, to form straps.

18. Join the bottom of the bib centrally behind the waistband, then stitch the ends of the straps at an angle behind the waist ties so that the inner edge of the strap is level with the end of the stitching on the ribbon. Pin, then fit the pinafore on the doll to check position is correct before sewing.

19. Cut a 20cm (8in) length of lace for each shoulder frill. Gather the straight edge and draw up to measure 7cm (2¾in). Beginning 2.5cm (1in) above the waistband, pin the gathered edge of the lace underneath the outer edge of the strap so that the frill extends over the shoulder as illustrated. Stitch in position, distributing gathers evenly and turning cut ends neatly under.

ALICE'S STRAPPED BLACK SHOES

20. Follow the directions given in Basics 10.

21. With the shoes on the doll, fit black ribbon over the foot. Pin the ribbon, at an angle on each side at the point marked with an O. Remove the shoe and cut the ribbon, allowing a 5–10mm (¼in) overlap. Stitch in place inside the shoe.

The Mad Hatter

One of fiction's best-loved crazy characters makes a most attractive doll, to give or to receive. He would add sartorial splendour to any nursery.

The Mad Hatter's enormously exaggerated wing collar is made from white felt that is glued to thin card in the version described below, because this is the simplest way to do it. However, you could also use the shirt fabric if you prefer and either glue it with dry-stick adhesive or bond it to the card with iron-on interfacing (Vilene Bondaweb).

Those dashing tartan trousers are just the thing for the fashionable Hatter but any small check would be equally smart. Just make sure that you match the design correctly, especially with a plaid fabric. If you are uncertain, here's a cutting out tip. Cut your first trouser piece, arranging the pattern on the fabric as you want the design to fall. Turn this piece over and place it on the remaining fabric, right sides together (or wrong sides together), so that the design on the fabric matches exactly. Pin the two layers together and cut the second piece using the first as your pattern.

The Hatter's elegant waistcoat has tiny buttons to match his trousers, but these should be omitted if the doll is intended for a very small child.

MATERIALS

Two 30cm (12in) squares of flesh-coloured felt

50g (2oz) ball of light-brown double-knit (Shetland style) yarn for hair

For other materials, see Basics 8, items 1–9 inclusive

23 × 65cm (9 × 25in) white cotton-type fabric, for shirt

30 × 45cm (12 × 18in) medium-weight small plaid or check fabric, for trousers

22 × 40cm (9 × 16in) orange felt, for legs

18cm (7in) square of white felt, for shirt collar

23 × 65cm (9 × 25in) mid-grey felt, for coat

11 × 24cm (4½ × 9½in) canary yellow felt, for waistcoast (vest)

35cm (⅜yd) black felt, 90cm (36in) wide, for hat and shoes

10cm (4in) square brown felt, for soles (optional)

50cm (½yd) silky white braid, 10mm (⅜in) wide, for shirt

60cm (⅝yd) very narrow gold braid, for waistcoat

25cm (¼yd) red grosgrain polka dot ribbon, 38mm (1½in) wide, for bow-tie

45cm (½yd) single-face black satin ribbon, 9mm (⅜in) wide, for hat

25cm (10in) single-face black satin ribbon, 6mm (¼in) wide, for shoes

15cm (6in) white bias binding, for shirt

60cm (¾yd) white narrow round elastic

20cm (¼yd) black narrow round elastic, for hat

5 snap-fasteners

3 small round orange beads (or tiny buttons), for waistcoat

10 × 18cm (4 × 7in) thin white card, for shirt collar

50cm (20in) square thin black card, for hat

10 × 7cm (4 × 2¾in) stiff white paper, for price ticket

Black felt pen, or alternative, for lettering

Matching threads

Dry-stick adhesive

Clear adhesive

THE MAD HATTER: BASIC FIGURE

Follow the directions for the basic Fairytale Doll on page 19, but cut the legs and soles in orange felt – or a suitable colour so that he will have socks to tone with his trousers.

Also, instead of the stitched nose which is described in step 11, use the pattern to cut a circle in flesh felt. Gather with tiny stitches very close to the edge, then partially draw up and put a small ball of stuffing in the centre. Draw up tightly and catch the edges together to give a smoothly rounded ball. Stitch or glue this to the centre of the face. For the Mad Hatter's hair, see Basics 9.

MAD HATTER'S WING-COLLARED SHIRT

1. Cut the shirt back once and the front and sleeve twice each, in fabric.
2. Join the front pieces to the back at shoulders.
3. Mark the centre at the top of the sleeve, then gather between the circles. Fit the sleeve into the armhole of the shirt, matching the side edges and notches and the centre top with the shoulder seam. Draw up the gathers to fit, distributing them evenly between the marked points, and stitch. Clip curves. When both sleeves are in place, join the side seams of the sleeves and body.
4. Make a narrow hem around the lower edge. Turn the front edges under as indicated by the broken line on the pattern and herringbone stitch over the raw edge.
5. Turn under the raw edge around the lower edge of each sleeve, then fold under along the broken line and stitch the hem. Now make a second line of stitches, 5mm (¼in) below the first, to form a narrow channel. Thread elastic through and draw up to fit the wrists.
6. Bind the neck neatly. Stitch snap-fasteners inside the front opening at neck, centre and waist.
7. Cut the collar in thin card. Glue to white felt and cut the felt level all round. Repeat to cover the other side of the card.
8. Matching the centre of the inner curve of the collar to the centre back of the neck, oversew the collar to the neck binding between the notches on the shirt front.
9. Glue white braid over the cut edge of the collar and down one shirt front, over the snap-fasteners.

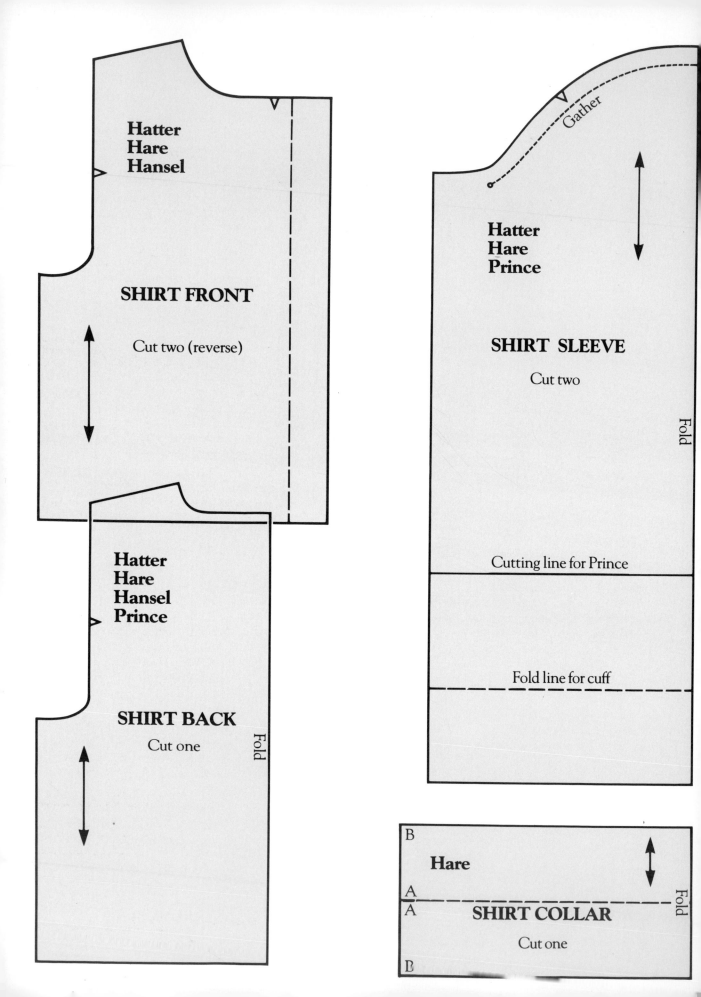

**Hatter
Hare
Hansel**

SHIRT FRONT

Cut two (reverse)

**Hatter
Hare
Hansel
Prince**

SHIRT BACK

Cut one

Fold

Gather

**Hatter
Hare
Prince**

SHIRT SLEEVE

Cut two

Fold

Cutting line for Prince

Fold line for cuff

B

Hare

A
A

Fold

SHIRT COLLAR

Cut one

B

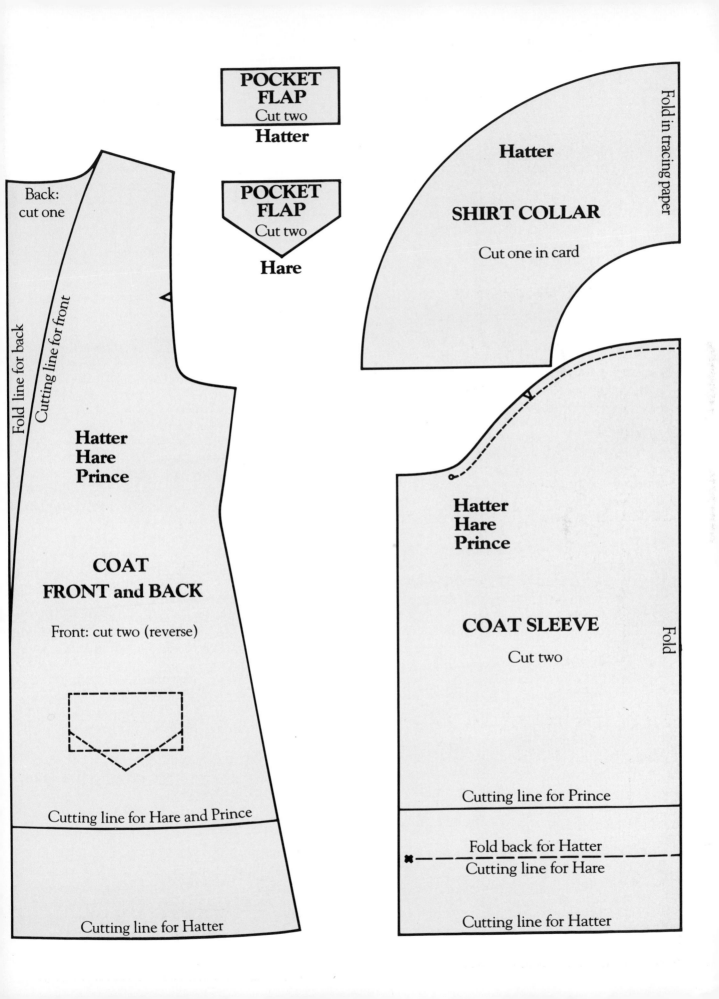

POCKET FLAP
Cut two
Hatter

POCKET FLAP
Cut two
Hare

Hatter
SHIRT COLLAR
Cut one in card

Fold in tracing paper

Back: cut one

Fold line for back

Cutting line for front

Hatter
Hare
Prince

COAT FRONT and BACK

Front: cut two (reverse)

Cutting line for Hare and Prince

Cutting line for Hatter

Hatter
Hare
Prince

COAT SLEEVE

Cut two

Fold

Cutting line for Prince

Fold back for Hatter

Cutting line for Hare

Cutting line for Hatter

MAD HATTER'S TARTAN TROUSERS

10. Follow the directions given in Basics 10.

MAD HATTER'S SPOTTED BOW-TIE

11. Make a formal bow (see Basics 6) from 20cm (7¾in) polka dot ribbon, binding the centre with a 2.5cm (1in) length folded widthways.
12. Fix the centre of a 15cm (6in) length of elastic to the back of the bow, then fit the elastic around the neck (inside collar) and tie ends at the back.

MAD HATTER'S CANARY YELLOW WAISTCOAT (VEST)

13. Cut the back once and the front twice, in yellow felt.
14. Oversew the front pieces to the back at each shoulder. Then join the side seams.
15. Stitch snap-fasteners inside the front opening at the points marked with an O.
16. Glue braid all round the outer edge, beginning at the top and ending at the bottom of the inside of the centre front opening. Stitch beads to outer centre front for buttons, as illustrated.

MAD HATTER'S GREY FROCK COAT

17. Cut the back once, and the front and sleeve twice each, in grey felt.
18. Oversew the front pieces to the back at each shoulder. (*Note:* For best results, sew this garment by hand.)
19. Fit the sleeves into the armholes of the coat as described in step 3 for his shirt, but gather close to the edge of the felt, and don't clip the curve. Oversew the side seams of the coat, and join the sleeves between the armhole and point X. Turn to the right side and finish sewing the sleeve seams on the outside, then turn back cuffs along the broken line. Press the cuffs, then open out the side seams of the coat and press flat.
20. Cut two pocket flaps and glue the top edges to the coat fronts as indicated on the pattern.

MAD HATTER'S TOP HAT

21. Cut the brim twice, and the side and crown once each, in thin black card (ignore the broken lines). Curve the side round and glue the overlap. Glue the two brim pieces together.
22. Using dry-stick adhesive, glue the top side of the brim to black felt, then trim the felt level with the inner and outer edges of the circles. Cover the under-side of the brim in the same way, but this time trim only the outer edge level with the card. Cut away a 6cm (2½in) circle of felt in the centre, as indicated by the broken line on the pattern. Now cut this surplus into small tabs, as indicated.
23. Place the side of the hat over the top of the brim, then very carefully glue the tabs up inside the hat so that the brim is held firmly in position (turn the whole thing upside down to do this).
24. Glue the crown to the felt, then cut away the felt to leave a 1.5cm (⅝in) overlap all round, as shown in the pattern. Cut V-shaped notches all round this surplus, as indicated.
25. Place the crown felt uppermost on top of the hat and carefully glue the tabs down all round the top edge of the side, so that the crown is held firmly in position.
26. Cut the side pattern again, but this time in felt, allowing about 5mm (¼in) extra around the top edge. Trail clear adhesive all round the hat close to the upper edge, over the tabs, and also around the lower edge, then trail a line from top to bottom. Beginning with one edge over this line, fit the felt smoothly round the hat, then glue the overlap. Trim away the excess felt at the top, level with the edge of the crown.
27. Knot both ends of the elastic and stitch inside the hat, at each side, adjusting the length as necessary so that it fits under the Hatter's hair to hold the hat in position (mould the top of his head into a more rounded shape to ensure that the hat fits properly – and you may prefer to catch the elastic at the sides and back of the head to hold the hat more permanently).
28. Fit 9mm (⅜in) ribbon around the side of the hat. Stitch or glue the ends where they meet, then cover the join with a small formal bow made from 8cm (3in) ribbon (see Basics 6, but don't bind the centre).
29. Trace and copy the price ticket onto stiff white paper, then slip into the ribbon band at one side of the hat, as illustrated.

MAD HATTER'S LACE-UP SHOES

30. Follow the directions given in Basics 10.
31. Make butterfly bows from 12.5cm (4¾in) lengths of 6mm (¼in) black ribbon (see Basics 6, mark points B 3.5cm (1⅜in) from A). Stitch or glue to the front of each shoe.

In this Style

10/6

PRICE TICKET

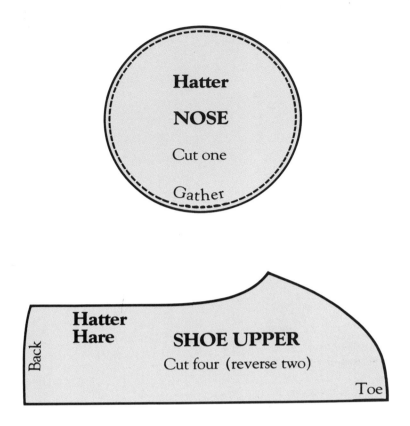

Hatter
NOSE

Cut one

Gather

Hatter Hare
SHOE UPPER

Cut four (reverse two)

Back

Toe

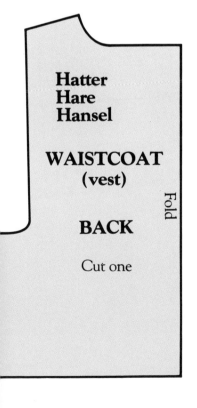

Hatter
Hare
Hansel

WAISTCOAT
(vest)

BACK

Cut one

Fold

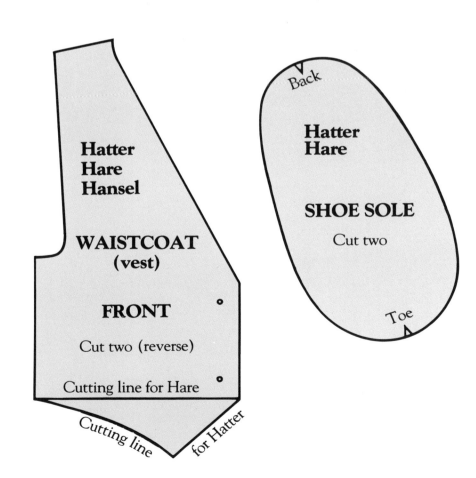

Hatter
Hare
Hansel

WAISTCOAT
(vest)

FRONT

Cut two (reverse)

Cutting line for Hare

Cutting line   for Hatter

Back

Hatter
Hare

SHOE SOLE

Cut two

Toe

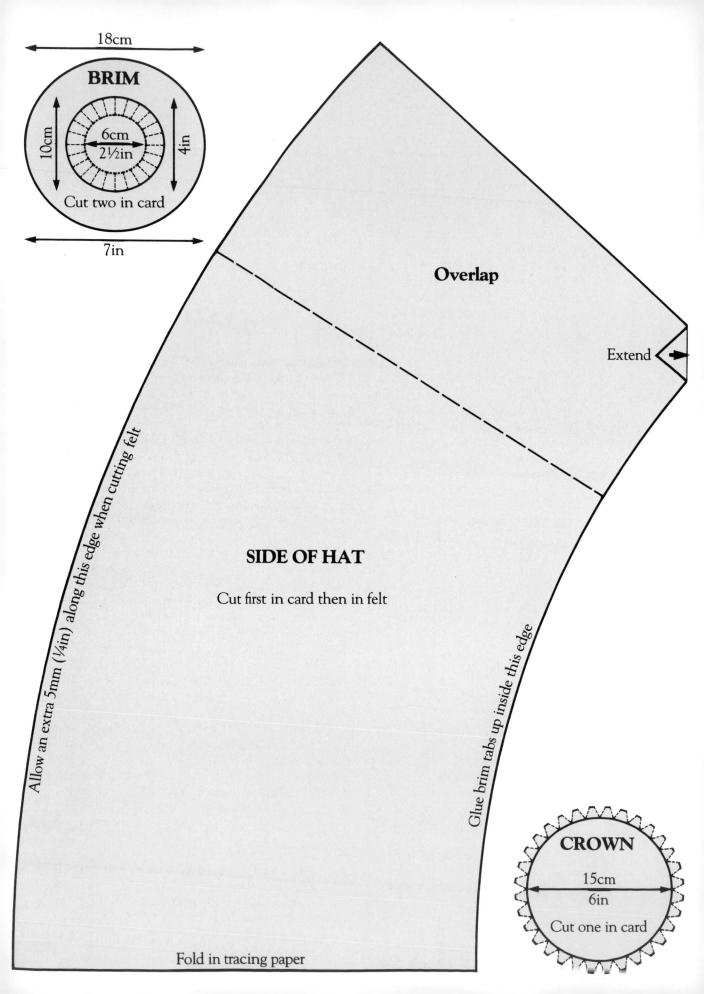

BRIM

18cm

10cm

6cm
2½in

4in

Cut two in card

7in

Overlap

Extend

SIDE OF HAT

Cut first in card then in felt

Allow an extra 5mm (¼in) along this edge when cutting felt

Glue brim tabs up inside this edge

CROWN

15cm

6in

Cut one in card

Fold in tracing paper

The March Hare

The Hatter's equally mad companion is a simple adaptation of the basic Fairytale Doll (see page 19). First you make the basic felt figure for the body (with a slight variation for the paws), then add an appropriate head made of brown towelling (you could, if you prefer, make the head in fur fabric, but choose one with a fairly close pile).

Instantly lovable, the March Hare is the perfect toy for young children, although his zany humour has special appeal for small boys. His warm personality makes him a cheerful day-time friend and a comforting bed-mate to be tucked up with on a dark night.

The March Hare's outfit is a country cousin version of the Hatter's fashionable image. When deciding the colour scheme for his outfit, the Hare was inspired by a bed of rhubarb! However, any tasteful combination of eye-catching colours would be equally suitable for this humorous toy. For this reason, felt amounts for the coat and shoes are given separately, in case you want to make them in different colours.

MATERIALS

Three 30cm (12in) squares of medium-to-dark brown felt

30cm (12in) matching brown towelling, 90cm (36in) wide

15 × 25cm (6 × 10in) stiff canvas or alternative interlining for ears

Scrap of black felt for nose

3 × 6cm (1¼ × 2½in) camel-colour felt for eyes

Stranded black embroidery cotton

For other materials, see Basics 8, items 1, 2, 5, 6, 7, 8, 9 and 10

23 × 65cm (9 × 25in) red-spotted, white cotton-type fabric for shirt

30 × 45cm (12 × 18in) medium-weight narrowly striped cotton-type fabric for trousers

20 × 65cm (8 × 25in) olive-green felt for coat

10 × 20cm (4 × 8in) olive-green felt for shoes

10cm (4in) square of beige felt for soles

11 × 24cm (4½ × 9½in) red felt for waistcoat (vest)

60cm (⅝yd) very narrow olive-green braid for waistcoat

10cm (4in) double-edge white lace, 10mm (⅜in) wide, for shirt (or 20cm/8in very narrow straight-edge)

20cm (8in) Apple Green grosgrain Swiss dot ribbon, 23mm (⅞in) wide, for bow-tie

25cm (10in) single-face satin ribbon, 9mm (⅜in) wide, to match shoes

60cm (¾yd) narrow round elastic

5 snap-fasteners

Matching threads

Clear adhesive

THE MARCH HARE: BASIC FIGURE

In towelling, and using the patterns given on page 61, cut the head twice (reverse the second piece) and the gusset once. Mark the mouth on both head pieces as follows: pin the pattern to the right side of the fabric and stick a pin straight down through the pattern and fabric every 3mm (⅛in) or so. Push the heads right down against the paper, then gently ease the pattern away to leave the pins stuck in the fabric. Using black sewing thread, back-stitch along this line, following the position of the pins very accurately and removing them as you sew.

Join the two head pieces between points A–B. Very carefully match the tip of the gusset (A) to the top of the seam, then join to each side of the head between points A–C. Join dart E–D. Turn up a narrow hem around the lower edge and gather, but don't draw up. Turn to the right side.

Stuff the head above the neck firmly and evenly to emphasise the shaping and to ensure that it is nicely rounded. Make sure that the sides are well filled, and when you have finished, push a little extra into the front between the nose and chin. Mould it with your hands, holding it up and looking straight at the face to make sure that the head is a good shape.

Using brown felt, follow the directions given on page 19 for the basic Fairytale Doll, adapting each step as follows:

Step 1: Omit the head and use the arm pattern on page 61.

Steps 2 and 3: Ignore.

Step 4: Make up the body as directed, then push the neck up inside the head until you have a 1cm (⅜in) overlap. Pin together, matching the centres at front and back, and notches to shoulder seams at each side. Draw up the gathers to fit, distributing them evenly, and stitch securely into place.

Step 5: Stiffen the neck as described, if necessary, then stuff the body to just below the waist.

Step 6: As directed, ignoring instructions for the thumb.

Steps 7, 8 and 9: As directed.

Step 10: Prepare the eyes as directed, using golden-yellow or light brown sequins. Then cut two more circles for the outer eye (see pattern opposite). Glue these behind the prepared eyes.

Step 11: Cut the nose (see pattern opposite) in black felt.

Step 12: Embroider the mouth in stem stitch over the marked line, using six strands of embroidery cotton. Then embroider a line, following the seam, between the centre of the mouth and the tip of the gusset.

Cut the ear pattern given opposite four times in towelling. Then cut two more pieces, following the broken line, in canvas.

For each ear, tack a piece of canvas to the wrong side of one ear: then right sides facing, join two towelling pieces together all round, leaving the straight lower edge open. Turn to the right side and turn the raw lower edge up inside, then oversew the two edges together. Fold the two lower corners over to meet at the centre of the lower edge and catch into position.

Pin the ears to the back of the head, positioning the centre of each ear over the gusset seam, and following the photograph for guidance. Stitch securely into place, using a darning needle and double thread.

Glue the nose to the tip of the gusset, then pin the eyes to the head to determine their position. When you are satisfied, glue them into place.

THE MARCH HARE'S SPOTTED SHIRT

1. Cut the shirt back and the straight collar once each, and the front and sleeve twice each, in spotted fabric.

2. Follow steps 2, 3, 4 and 5 for making the Mad Hatter's shirt.

3. With right sides together and centres matching, stitch one long edge of the collar around the neck, allowing it to overlap the front edges of the shirt 5mm (1/4in) at each end. With right side inside, fold the collar in half as indicated by the broken line on the pattern, then stitch each end between points A–B. Clip corners and turn the collar to the right side. Turn the raw edge under and slip stitch the lower edge of the collar inside the shirt.

4. Stitch snap-fasteners inside the front opening at neck, centre and waist, but have the top one 1cm (3/8in) below the collar, to allow the collar to set properly.

5. Stitch lace down the centre front of the shirt.

THE MARCH HARE'S STRIPED TROUSERS

6. Follow the directions given in Basics 10.

THE MARCH HARE'S SWISS DOT BOW-TIE

7. Follow the directions (steps 11–12) for the Mad Hatter's bow-tie, but use only 16.5cm (6½in) ribbon, bound as described. When you fit the tie, put the elastic over the shirt. Fold the collar over the elastic at the back, but allow the corners to stand up at the front.

THE MARCH HARE'S RED WAISTCOAT (VEST)

8. Follow the directions (steps 13–16) for the Mad Hatter's waistcoat, omitting the bead buttons. Note the cutting line for the front.

THE MARCH HARE'S OLIVE-GREEN FROCK COAT

9. Follow the directions (steps 17–20) for the Mad Hatter's frock coat, noting the shorter cutting lines for the coat and sleeves, and the alternative pattern for the pocket flaps. Ignore the instructions for the cuffs (step 22).

THE MARCH HARE'S LACE-UP SHOES

10. Follow the directions given in Basics 10, using green felt for the uppers and beige for the soles. Then make bows from matching ribbon as described for the Mad Hatter (step 31).

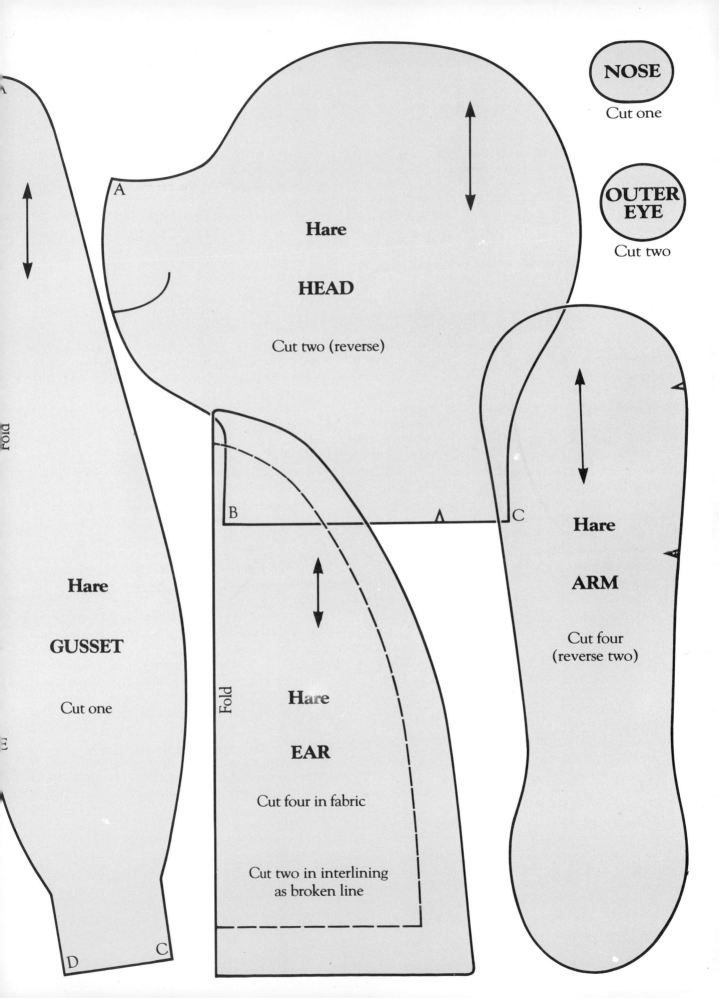

NOSE

Cut one

OUTER EYE

Cut two

A

Hare

HEAD

Cut two (reverse)

Fold

Hare

GUSSET

Cut one

D   C

B   A   C

Fold

Hare

EAR

Cut four in fabric

Cut two in interlining
as broken line

Hare

ARM

Cut four
(reverse two)

The Dormouse

Lewis Carroll never made it quite clear whether the Dormouse was bemused or bored by the senseless conversation of his companions at the tea-table. But whatever the reason for his drowsiness, it seems very unfair that the Hatter and the Hare found it necessary to stuff the harmless little creature into the teapot!

Soft and round and cuddly, the Dormouse would have a much happier life in the comfortable surroundings of a baby's cot or pram, and even if he did get thrown out every now and again, he's so well cushioned, it wouldn't hurt. On the other hand, he'd make a very restful companion sitting sleepily on a shelf – perhaps beside your sewing-machine as a helpful pincushion (although that might seem an even worse fate than being stuffed into a teapot).

This versatile little character is so quick and inexpensive to make that he is an ideal subject if you have money-making enterprises in mind. Although this version is in authentic dormouse soft brown, you could make your own designer collection of colourful mice in every shade of the rainbow, perhaps even with contrast ears and tail. A decoration of embroidered or lace flowers scattered over his round little body would add a charming touch, too.

If the mouse is to be used for decorative purposes, it will sit better if it has a stiff card base: but if it is intended for a baby's use, stiffen the underside with canvas or a heavy non-woven interlining so that it will be completely washable.

MATERIALS

25cm (10in) square soft mid-brown felt
Scrap of black felt
30cm (12in) matching lacing cord
Polyester stuffing
Stiffening for base (see above)
Matching and black threads
Clear adhesive

1. Cut the gusset and the base once each, the head and body twice each, and the ear four times. Cut the base once more, following the broken line, in card, canvas or interlining. Mark the notches carefully.
2. Gather each body piece as indicated with tiny stitches close to the edge. Pin each body piece to a head piece, matching the notches. Draw up the gathers to fit, distributing them evenly, and oversew neatly together.
3. Join the two head pieces between points A–B. Match the tip of the gusset (A) to the top of the seam and oversew very carefully to each side of the head, continuing to match the edge of the gusset to the edge of the head and body between points A–C–D. Turn to the right side.
4. Glue card stiffening to the felt base, or tack canvas or interlining to the felt. Then, with the stiffening inside, fit the base inside the lower edge of the mouse, matching the centre front and back points. Oversew very neatly together, leaving the back open between the points marked with an X.
5. Stuff well, making sure that you push the filling well into the nose and face. Mould the body into a softly rounded ball, and when the stuffing is complete, slip stitch the opening.
6. Make a tiny hole at the centre back of the gusset, just above the base, at point marked with an O. Tie a knot at one end of the lacing cord. Push the knot inside the hole, then stitch neatly to close the edges of the hole around the cord and hold it in position. Smear a little adhesive onto the other cut end of the cord, then roll it smoothly into a point with your fingertips.
7. For each ear, oversew two pieces together with tiny stitches, leaving the straight lower edges open. Gather very neatly along this edge and draw up to measure 2–2.5cm (¾–1in). Curve the ears around and pin them to the top of the head, centrally over the gusset seams, as illustrated. Stitch securely into position.
8. Embroider a curved line for each eye as indicated on the pattern, as follows. Using black sewing thread, embroider the curve in stem stitch. Embroider a second line, beginning and ending at the same points as the first, but stitching the line itself underneath, alongside and against, the first curve. Embroider a third line in exactly the same way (see diagram).
9. Cut the nose in black felt and glue to the tip of the gusset.

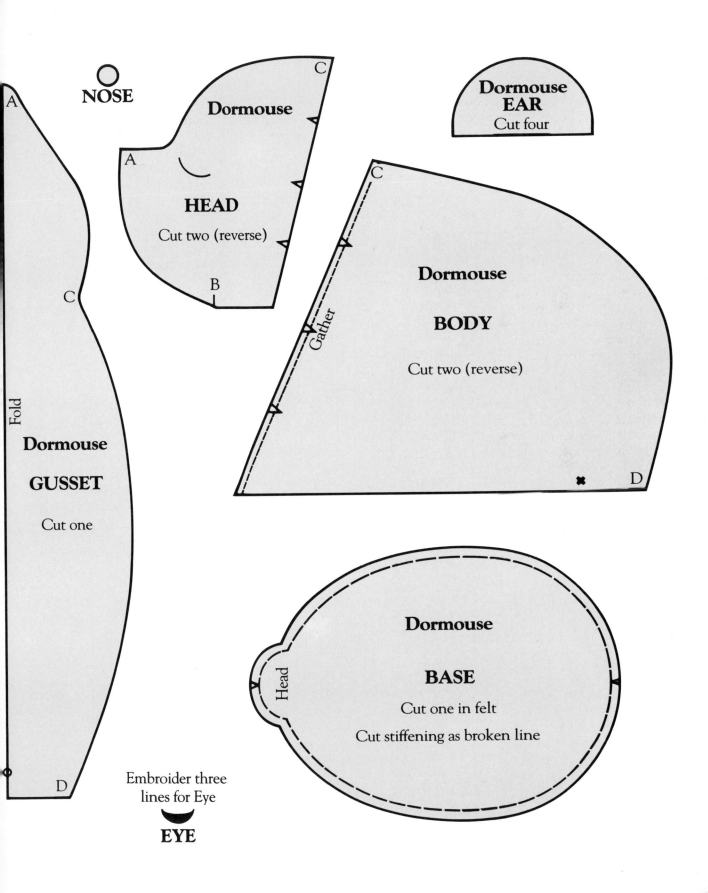

NOSE

Dormouse

A

A

HEAD

Cut two (reverse)

B

C

Dormouse EAR

Cut four

C

Dormouse

BODY

Cut two (reverse)

Gather

D

Fold

C

Dormouse

GUSSET

Cut one

D

Embroider three
lines for Eye

EYE

Head

Dormouse

BASE

Cut one in felt

Cut stiffening as broken line

CHAPTER 3

The Kingdom of Sweets

Baby Bear trudged on. He was bored with walking. 'Can I have a chocolate bar?' he asked his mother dejectedly.

'Of course not,' she replied quickly. 'It's far too near lunch!'

'If it's the wrong time for *eating* sweets,' said Father Bear cheerfully, 'let's have a story about them instead!'

Baby Bear didn't think much of this idea. 'Which story?' he asked.

'The Nutcracker!' laughed his father.

This is about a little girl called Clara who is given a nutcracker made to look like a toy soldier. Then the toy soldier turns into a real prince and takes Clara through the Land of Snow and Ice to the Kingdom of Sweets. Clara sits on a golden throne and the handsome prince dances with the beautiful Sugar Plum Fairy, with whom he falls in love.

Baby Bear forgot his tired legs as he thought of all the tempting treats in the Kingdom of Sweets. Then he saw the brown butterfly again, fluttering among the leaves above his head. And there was snow on the trees, and pink and white candies hanging from the branches.

Now he could see Clara, sitting on her throne, and the soldier-prince was dancing with the prettiest fairy in Fairyland. Mother Bear followed Baby Bear quietly and Clara turned to greet them. Baby Bear watched the dancers as they swirled and twirled together in each other's arms, and suddenly he wanted to dance too. He wriggled down from the throne and tried a few ballet steps of his own. Then there was a bump and he was sitting on the ground feeling very sorry for himself. Looking up he saw the butterfly. 'Wait for me!' he cried, clambering up and scampering after it.

'I've been to the Kingdom of Sweets!' he shouted. 'And I danced with the Sugar Plum Fairy.'

'Yes, dear, I know,' said Mother Bear. 'But don't wander off like that again; we have to stop and look for you.'

'Grown-ups are impossible,' sighed Baby Bear as he followed his parents along the path. 'They never get excited about *anything*!'

Clara

Clara looks so demure and pretty in her chemise and lace-trimmed pantalettes. Clara, the young heroine in *The Nutcracker* ballet, wears an old-fashioned party frock in dark olive green, with a vivid heliotrope rose at the waist to match the larger one in her hair.

The high waistline means that the lower part of the armhole is set into the skirt, but this is easy to do if you follow the diagrams and instructions.

MATERIALS

Three 30cm (12in) squares of flesh-coloured felt
50g (2oz) ball soft brown double-knit yarn for hair
For other materials, see Basics 8, items 1–9 inclusive

30cm (12in) medium-weight olive-green cotton-type fabric, 90cm (36in) wide
30cm (12in) light-weight white cotton-type fabric, 90cm (36in) wide, for chemise and pantalettes
12 × 20cm (4½ × 8in) black felt for dancing pumps
1.75m (1⅞yd) heavy (guipure) lace, 10mm (⅜in) deep, to trim chemise and pantalettes
1.6m (1¾yd) white lace, 20mm (¾in) deep, to trim dress
80cm (⅞yd) double-edge white lace, 10mm (⅜in) wide, to trim dress
40cm (½yd) single-face satin ribbon, 6mm (¼in) wide, to match the dress
35cm (14in) single-face satin ribbon, 6mm (¼in) wide, in contrast colour, for roses
70cm (⅞yd) narrow round elastic
2 snap-fasteners
Matching threads

CLARA: THE BASIC FIGURE

Follow the directions for the basic Fairytale Doll on page 19. As for Alice, you could if you liked, give her black stockings under her dainty pantalettes – just cut the legs and soles in black felt instead of flesh-colour. For Clara's hair, see Basics 9.

CLARA'S CHEMISE AND PANTALETTES

1. Cut a piece of fabric 25cm (10in) deep × 40cm (16in) wide, for the chemise. Cut the pantalettes pattern twice.
2. Join the side edges of the chemise for the centre back seam. Turn under the raw top edge, then make a 5mm (¼in) hem around the top. Thread elastic through this hem and draw up to fit the body just above the bust.
3. Fit the chemise on the doll. Cut two 7cm (2¾in) lengths of lace and pin them to the top edge, each 2cm (¾in) from the centre front of the chemise. Then take the lace over the shoulders to form straps and pin them into position at the back. Stitch into place.
4. Make a very narrow hem around the lower edge and then trim with lace, just overlapping the edge.
5. Follow the directions given in Basics 10 to make the pantalettes.

CLARA'S HIGH-WAISTED PARTY FROCK

6. Cut a piece of fabric 28cm (11in) deep × 30cm (12in) wide for the skirt front, and two pieces 28 × 15cm (11 × 6in) for the skirt back. Place the armhole pattern on each top corner of the front and cut round it. Do the same thing at the outer top corner only of the skirt back pieces. Then cut the bodice front once, and the back and sleeve twice each.
7. Join the bodice front to the back pieces at each shoulder.
8. Mark the top edge of the skirt front equally into four, then gather. Pin to the lower edge of the bodice front, side edges level, matching the marked points to the notches. Draw up to fit, then stitch, distributing the gathers evenly. Turn the seam up behind the bodice and tack.

Join the skirt back pieces to the bodice back in the same way, but begin by gathering 2cm (¾in) in from the centre back edge. Mark the centre of the top edge of the skirt and match it to the notch.
9. Mark the centre at the top edge of the sleeve, then gather between the circles. Fit the sleeve into the armhole, matching the side edges and notches, and centre top with the shoulder seam. Draw up the gathers to fit, distributing them evenly between the marked points, and stitch. Clip curves. When both sleeves are in place, join the side seams of the sleeves and skirt.
10. Join the centre back seam of the skirt, leaving 8cm (3in) open at the top. Turn under the centre back edges of the bodice as indicated by the broken

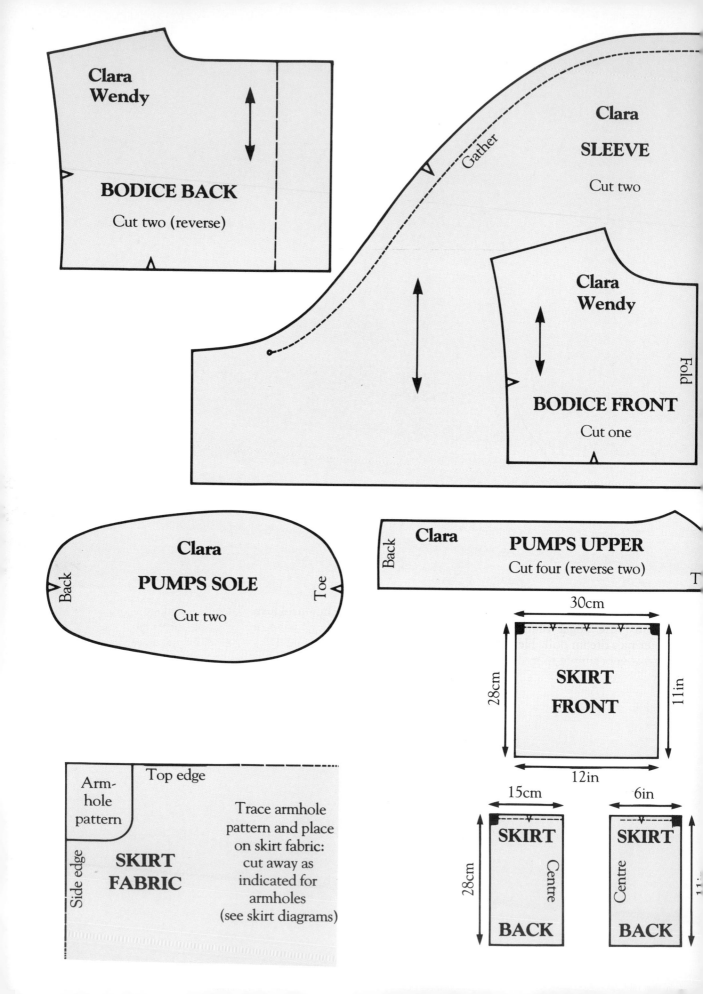

**Clara
Wendy**

BODICE BACK

Cut two (reverse)

Gather

**Clara
SLEEVE**

Cut two

**Clara
Wendy**

Fold

BODICE FRONT

Cut one

**Clara
PUMPS SOLE**

Back

Toe

Cut two

Back

Clara

PUMPS UPPER

Cut four (reverse two)

T

30cm

28cm

**SKIRT
FRONT**

11in

12in

Top edge

Arm-
hole
pattern

Side edge

**SKIRT
FABRIC**

Trace armhole
pattern and place
on skirt fabric:
cut away as
indicated for
armholes
(see skirt diagrams)

15cm

6in

28cm

SKIRT

Centre

BACK

Centre

SKIRT

BACK

11

line and stitch. Turn under the edges of the skirt opening to correspond.

11. Bind the neck edge neatly, then stitch narrow double-edge lace over the binding.

12. Stitch snap-fasteners to the back opening at the neck and waist.

13. Turn under the raw edge around the lower edge of each sleeve, then make a 1cm (⅜in) hem. Trim with wide lace, stitching the top edge of the lace to the very edge of the sleeve, so that the lace overlaps below. Be sure to leave the sleeve hem at least 6–7mm (¼in) wide. Thread elastic through this channel and draw up to fit the arm.

14. Turn up and stitch a hem around the skirt (about 3.5cm/1⅜in) but fit the dress on the doll to check length. Stitch a band of wide lace around the hem, the top edge 3.5cm (1⅜in) above the edge of the skirt. Stitch a band of narrow double-edge lace 1cm (⅜in) above the first row.

15. Cut a length of narrow toning ribbon 1cm (⅜in) more than the width of the lower edge of the bodice. Turn the cut ends under and pin across the bodice, lower edges of bodice and ribbon level. Stitch at each side, against the sleeve, and at the centre.

Fold a 30cm (12in) length of the same ribbon in half and catch the fold to the centre of the waistband.

Make a rose (see Basics 6) from 14–15cm (5½–6in) contrast 6mm (¼in) ribbon, and stitch over the top of streamers.

CLARA'S RIBBONS AND LACE HAIR TRIM

16. Make a butterfly bow from the wide toning ribbon (see Basics 6. Mark points B 9cm (3½in) each side of point A).

17. Cut a 40cm (16in) length of wide lace and gather the straight edge for 5cm (2in) at the centre. Draw up tightly and secure gathers, then stitch the gathered area over the centre of the bow, so that the lace streamers hang down between the ribbon ones.

18. Make a rose from 20cm (8in) ribbon, and stitch at the centre of the lace.

19. Stitch the bow to the crown of her head.

CLARA'S BLACK DANCING PUMPS

20. Follow the directions given in Basics 10.

The Sugar Plum Fairy

All frothy frills, gleaming pearls and sparkling sequins, the Sugar Plum Fairy is every aspiring ballerina's dream doll. Her shimmering lilac satin dress is very simple to make. Buy a soft lining satin rather than dress satin, which is not only more expensive, but too stiff. Then you just need time to make all those romantic butterfly bows and satin roses.

MATERIALS

Three 30cm (12in) squares of flesh-coloured felt
50g (2oz) ball dark brown double-knit yarn for hair
For other materials, see Basics 8, page 19, items 1–9 inclusive.

35cm (14in) lilac lining satin, 90cm (36in) wide
65cm (¾yd) pink net, 120cm (48in) wide *and* 50cm (⅝yd) white net, 120cm (48in) wide *or* use all pink
10cm (4in) square lilac felt, for shoes
9cm (3½in) square beige felt, for shoes
50cm (½yd) Rosy Mauve feather-edge satin ribbon, 16mm (⅝in) wide
4m (4½yd) Rosy Mauve single-face satin ribbon, 9mm (⅜in) wide
2.5m (2¾yd) Light Orchid single-face satin ribbon, 9mm (⅜in) wide
1.2m (1⅜yd) Light Orchid double-face satin ribbon, 3mm (⅛in) wide
20cm (¼yd) metallic silver ribbon, 16mm (⅝in) wide
2m (2¼yd) white lace, 10mm (⅜in) deep
50cm (⅝yd) tiny pearl bead trimming
10 medium (about 10mm/⅜in) tear-drop pearl beads
Small silver star sequins (at least 50)
1.2m (1⅜yd) lilac bias binding
50cm (½yd) narrow round elastic
2 snap-fasteners
Matching threads
Clear adhesive

THE SUGAR PLUM FAIRY: THE BASIC FIGURE

Follow the directions for the basic Fairytale Doll on page 19, using blue sequins for the eyes. For the Sugar Plum Fairy's hair, see Basics 9.

SUGAR PLUM FAIRY'S BALLET DRESS

1. Cut a strip of satin 22cm (8½in) deep × 90cm (36in) wide for the skirt. Then cut the bodice front once and the back and panties twice each. Cut two strips of net, one in each colour, 40cm (16in) deep × 120cm (48in) wide, for the over-skirt, and cut two strips of pink net, 14 × 60cm (5½ × 24in), for the bodice frills.

2. Make the panties, following the directions given in Basics 10.

3. Join the bodice front to the back pieces at each side (stitch these seams twice more, over the seam allowance, for added strength and to prevent fraying – and don't worry about opening out the seam).

4. Mark the top edge of the skirt equally into

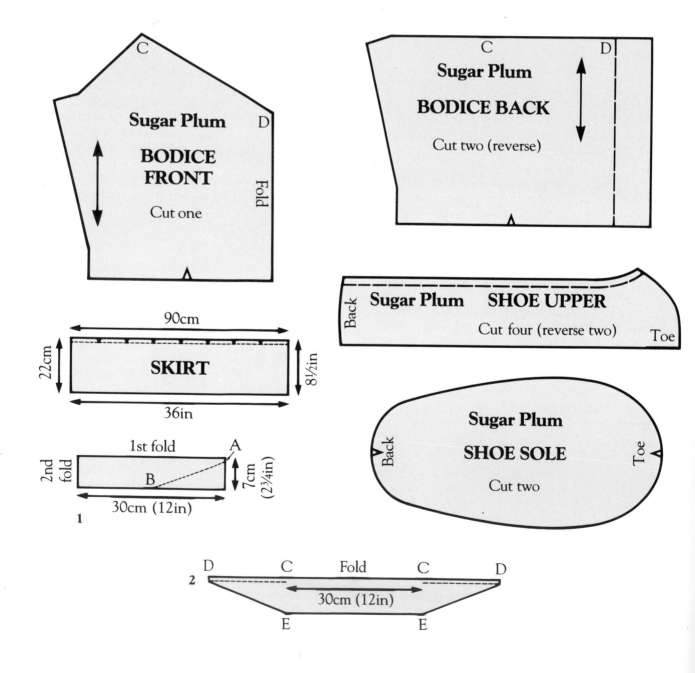

eight. Beginning and ending 2cm (¾in) from the side edges, gather along the top edge. With right sides together, pin the skirt to the lower edge of the bodice, side edges level and matching the marked points to notches and seams: draw up gathers to fit, distributing them evenly between the pins, then stitch securely (oversew the raw edges to strengthen and prevent fraying).

5. Join the centre back seam of skirt, leaving 8cm (3in) open at the top for the back opening. Turn under the raw lower edge and stitch, then make a hem so that the skirt length is 18cm (7in) all round.

6. Turn under the raw edges at each side of the centre back opening, then fold under along the broken line and stitch. Bind the top edge of the bodice. Fit the dress on the doll and mark the position of snap-fasteners on the centre back opening at the top and waist. Stitch into position.

7. For the bodice frills, fold each strip of net in half lengthways, then in half across the first fold (figure 1). Mark A 1cm (⅜in) below the top edge, and B at the centre of the bottom edge. Cut along the broken line. Open out the second fold only, then mark C on the top edge 15cm (6in) from each end directly above points B (figure 2).

Use one piece for each side of the neck. Gather close to the top edge between points D–C, then pin D to the binding at the centre front of the bodice, and C to point C on the pattern. Draw up to fit and oversew to the edge of the binding, distributing the gathers evenly. Gather the other end in the same way between points C–D and pin to bodice back as indicated on the pattern. Draw up the gathers to fit and oversew to the bodice as before. Stitch the remaining central section of the top edge of the frill about 3–4mm (⅛in) below the fold: do not draw up. Thread elastic through the channel and draw up to fit over shoulders, knotting and securing the ends of the elastic very securely inside the bodice.

Stitch lace along the lower edge of the top layer of net. Catch points B together under each arm.

8. For the overskirt, place one piece of net on top of the other and tack one long edge. Measure 20cm (8in) between the top and bottom edges for the centre-line, marking with pins. Using a double thread and your darning needle, gather along this line. Mark the gathered line at four equal intervals with a coloured thread. Fold in half along the centre-line, but turn the layers of net over so that you have two white layers underneath and two pink layers on top. Pin the net over the skirt, the side edges over the centre back seam, and the marked points matching the side seams and centre front of the bodice. Draw up the gathers to fit, distributing them evenly, then catch securely into place immediately below the lower edge of the bodice. Join the edges of each layer of net at the centre back, leaving 5cm (2in) open at the top.

9. Make fifteen butterfly bows from 8cm (3in) lengths of 9mm (⅜in) Rosy Mauve ribbon (see Basics 6: mark points B 2.5cm (1in) from A). Stitch close together around the neckline. Make 31 similar Light Orchid bows to trim the overskirt as follows. Pin one bow at the centre front of the top layer of net, 4cm (1½in) above the bottom edge; pin another bow 6cm (2⅜in) above the first one, and another 6cm (2⅜in) above that. Pin three more bows at each side of the first bow, 11cm (4⅜in) apart, and all 4cm (1½in) from the bottom edge. Pin two more bows vertically above these, 6cm (2⅜in) apart as before, but omit the top bow at each side of the skirt (making only five in the top row). Now pin a bow between each vertical row, 7cm (2¾in) above the bottom edge; pin a second bow 6cm (2⅜in) above each of these. When you are satisfied with the position of all the bows, stitch them securely into place. Then glue sequins between all the bows on the skirt, and here and there on the bodice frill.

10. Make a bow at the centre of the feather-edge ribbon, then stitch at centre back of waist, over the lower snap-fastener.

SUGAR PLUM FAIRY'S HEAD-DRESS

11. Cut an 18cm (7in) length of silver ribbon. Stitch lace on top so that it overlaps the top edge by about 6mm (¼in). Curve round into a circle and glue a 1cm (⅜in) overlap.

12. Cut ten 5cm (2in) lengths of pearl trimming. Make each into a loop and bind the cut ends tightly together with thread between the first and second beads. Glue the tied ends to the back of the ribbon, evenly distanced apart, so that each loop stands about 1cm (⅜in) above the lace.

13. Make ten roses (see Basics 6) from 25cm (10in) lengths of 9mm (⅜in) wide ribbon. Position them evenly round the circlet between the pearl loops, stitching the centre of the base of each rose over the lower edge of the ribbon.

14. Stitch tear-drop pearls between the roses as follows: make a knot at the end of your thread, then surround it with a small blob of glue. Pass your needle up through the broad end of the pearl,

then stitch it to the lower edge of the ribbon, leaving enough slack to allow the pearl to hang attractively. (If you prefer, the thread may be held in place with a very tiny plain glass or pearl bead under the tear-drop.)

15. Fit the circlet over the Sugar Plum Fairy's top-knot (catch through the yarn to hold in place, if necessary).

SUGAR PLUM FAIRY'S BALLET SHOES

16. Cut the upper four times in lilac felt and the sole twice in beige.

17. Stitch the binding to the top edge of each upper, but before turning it over, cut away 2–3mm (⅛in) along the top edge of the felt and binding, as the broken line on the pattern indicates. Complete the binding.

18. For each shoe, join two uppers, oversewing at the front and back. Pin the lower edge to the sole, matching the seams to notches, then oversew. Turn to the right side.

19. Cut the 3mm (⅛in) ribbon in half for ties, and stitch the centre of each piece inside the top edge at the centre back of each shoe. Trim the front of each shoe with a Rosy Mauve bow.

The Nutcracker
Toy Soldier Prince

When they're on parade, he's the smartest soldier in the regiment – but of course, he's really a prince! No wonder the Sugar Plum Fairy falls in love with him.

That smoothly tailored uniform fits so perfectly because the garments are sewn to the doll itself. But if you want to remove his clothes, the stitches can easily be pulled out.

A striking colour combination is all-important. Here the soldier wears a mid-blue tunic faced with deep gold, above very pale blue-grey breeches.

Lampshade trimmings are your best hunting ground for a suitable braid to trim the uniform and helmet (see Basics 5). The very narrow black braid is made from plaited ribbon (see Basics 6), and you could use this method for the gold braid too – perhaps using a metallic gold ribbon: one plait would do for the narrow width, with two or more glued side by side for the helmet trimming and chin-strap.

A 50g (2oz) ball of yarn is specified for the hair, because double-knit yarn is not usually sold in smaller amounts. But if you are making the Sugar Plum Fairy too, you will find that one ball is enough for both hairstyles.

MATERIALS

Three 30cm (12in) squares of flesh-coloured felt

50g (2oz) ball of dark brown double-knit yarn for hair
For other materials, see Basics 8, items 1–4 and 6–9

30cm (12in) mid-blue felt, 90cm (36in) wide
22 × 35cm (8½ × 14in) pale-blue felt, for breeches
Two 20cm (8in) squares of deep gold felt
3cm (1¼in) diameter circle of light gold felt
25cm (10in) square black felt for boots
80cm (⅞yd) silky gold lampshade braid, about 10mm (⅜in) wide
1.35m (1½yd) silky gold braid, about 5mm (³⁄₁₆in) wide
or 70cm (¾yd) of the 10mm (⅜in) braid cut down the centre
30cm (12in) matching silky fringe, 2.5cm (1in) deep
9.5m (10¼yd) black satin ribbon, 1.5mm (¹⁄₁₆in) wide
2.25m (2½in) white satin ribbon, 1.5mm (¹⁄₁₆in) wide
Small black lace daisy or similar motif to trim helmet
Matching threads
30 × 45cm (12 × 18in) thin card
Dry-stick adhesive
Clear adhesive

THE TOY SOLDIER: BASIC FIGURE

Follow the directions for the basic Fairytale Doll on page 19, but omit the mouth (step 12). For the Toy Soldier's hair, see Basics 9.

THE TOY SOLDIER'S PALE-BLUE FELT BREECHES

1. Follow the directions given under Basics 10.

THE TOY SOLDIER'S HIGH BLACK BOOTS

2. Cut the upper four times (reversing two pieces), and the sole twice, in black felt.

3. To make each boot, oversew two uppers together at the front, from top to toe. Join the back only between the notch and the lower edge. Pin the lower edge to the sole, matching the seams to notches, then oversew. Turn to the right side.

4. Fit boots on the doll, over the breeches, pinning the back edges so that they overlap about 3mm (⅛in). Stitch the overlap neatly.

THE TOY SOLDIER'S TUNIC

5. Cut the back, front and sleeve twice each, and the collar once, in blue felt. Cut the front facing once, the tail lining and cuff twice each, and the epaulette four times, in gold felt.

6. Oversew the two back pieces together between the neck and notch, to form the centre back seam. Then glue the tail linings to the wrong side, trimming the cut edges level. Join the two lining pieces together at the top, above the notch. Make a tassel (see Basics 6) from 25cm (10in) black ribbon, folded into four and trimmed to measure 2cm (¾in). Stitch to the right side, at the base of the centre back seam.

7. Oversew the front pieces to the back at each shoulder.

8. Mark the centre at the top of the sleeve, then

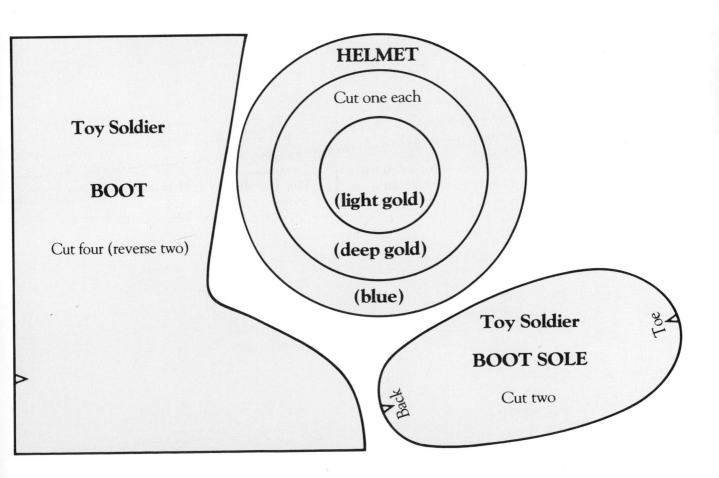

Toy Soldier

BOOT

Cut four (reverse two)

HELMET

Cut one each

(light gold)

(deep gold)

(blue)

Toy Soldier

BOOT SOLE

Cut two

Back

Toe

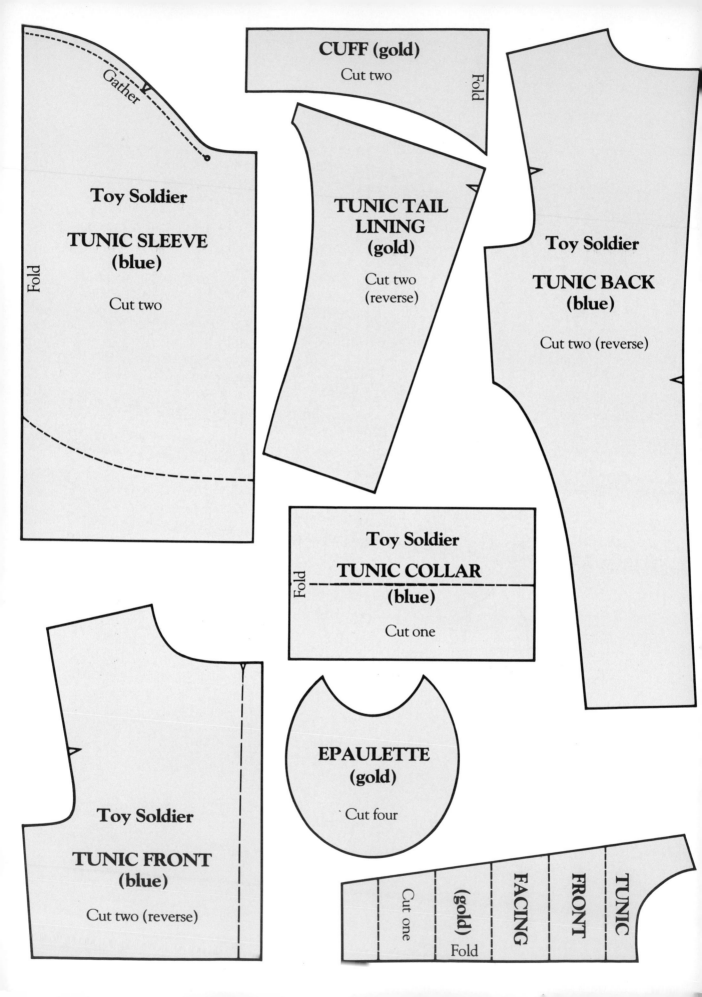

Toy Soldier

TUNIC SLEEVE (blue)

Gather

Fold

Cut two

CUFF (gold)

Cut two

Fold

TUNIC TAIL LINING (gold)

Cut two (reverse)

Toy Soldier

TUNIC BACK (blue)

Cut two (reverse)

Toy Soldier

TUNIC COLLAR (blue)

Fold

Cut one

Toy Soldier

TUNIC FRONT (blue)

Cut two (reverse)

EPAULETTE (gold)

Cut four

TUNIC FRONT FACING (gold) Fold Cut one

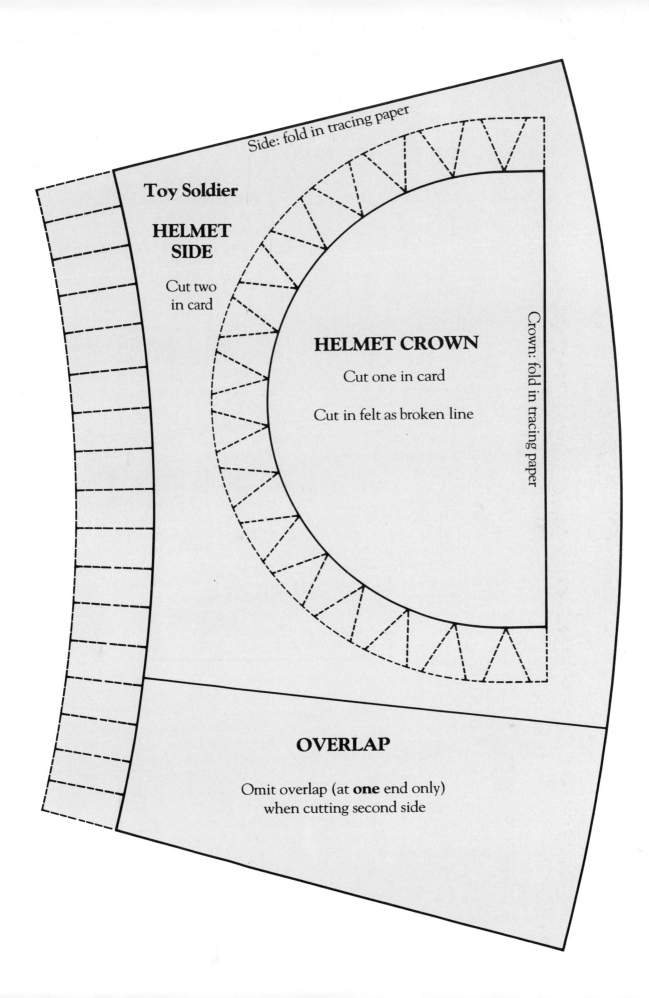

Toy Soldier

HELMET SIDE

Cut two in card

Side: fold in tracing paper

HELMET CROWN

Cut one in card

Cut in felt as broken line

Crown: fold in tracing paper

OVERLAP

Omit overlap (at **one** end only) when cutting second side

gather close to the edge between the circles. Fit the sleeve into the armhole of the tunic, matching the side edges and notches, and the centre top with the shoulder seam. Draw up the gathers to fit, then oversew together. When both the sleeves are in place, glue a cuff to the right side of each, side and lower edges level. Then join the side seams of the sleeves and body.

9. With right sides together and centres matching, oversew one long edge of the collar around the neck, between the notches. With the wrong side inside, fold the collar in half as indicated by the broken line on the pattern, then slip stitch the long edge inside the tunic, over the previous stitching line. Oversew the two ends neatly.

10. Glue narrow gold braid along the top and front edges of the collar and around the top edge of each cuff.

11. Fit the tunic on the doll, overlapping the front edges as indicated by the broken lines on the pattern. Pin, adjusting to fit if necessary, then stitch into place.

12. Prepare the front facing as follows. Mark the horizontal lines indicated on the pattern. Make a length of plaited braid (see Basics 6) from three 1.25m (46in) lengths of black ribbon. Glue this over the marked lines, stitching carefully at each end to prevent the braid from unravelling. Make ten tassels from 15cm (6in) black ribbon, folded into three, and trimmed to measure just over 1cm (just under ½in). Glue a tassel at both ends of each row of braid. Pin the facing to the front of the tunic, then stitch into position all round. Glue narrow gold braid along the lower edge.

13. To make each epaulette, stitch a fringe around the outer curved edge of one piece of felt, so that the top of the fringe covers the felt, and the fringe itself overlaps the edge. Place the second piece on top and stitch together all round. Glue narrow gold braid around the outer edge. Pin over each shoulder of the tunic, the inner curved edge level with the base of the collar, and stitch securely into position.

THE TOY SOLDIER'S HELMET

14. Cut the helmet side in thin card (ignore the broken lines), then cut again, but this time omit the overlap. Curve the first piece around and fix the overlap with paper clips. Place on doll to check size: it should fit loosely. Glue the overlap.

15. Cut the crown in card. Cut again in blue felt, following the outer broken line. Using stick adhesive, glue the card in the centre of the felt.

Snip the overlapping felt into V-shaped notches, as indicated. Place the crown over the helmet and glue the felt tabs down over the side all the way round.

16. Glue the second side piece to blue felt. Trim the top edge level with the card, but leave a 3cm (1¼in) overlap on one side edge, and a 2cm (¾in) overlap around the lower edge, as the broken line indicates on the pattern. Glue this side piece over the first one, top edges level, and overlap the felt at the back to join. Snip the surplus around the lower edge into small tabs, as indicated on the pattern, and glue them neatly up inside the helmet. Glue wider gold braid around the top, folding it over the edge.

17. Use the patterns to cut circles of blue, deep gold and light gold felt. Glue narrow gold braid around the edge of the blue circle. Make plaited braid from three 25cm (10in) lengths of black ribbon to edge the larger gold circle. Edge the smaller gold circle as the blue one; glue lace motif or alternative in the centre of this circle. Glue the circles together, centres matching. Finally, glue to the centre front of the helmet, 1cm (⅜in) below the braid trimming the top edge.

18. Make a length of braid from three 25cm (10in) lengths of plaited ribbon. Make two tassels, using 75cm (30in) black ribbon folded into eight, and trimmed to measure 3cm (1¼in). Loop the plait under the circle and stitch the ends into position as illustrated, 3cm (1¼in) each side of the centre circle. Stitch tassels on top.

19. Make three more tassels as step 18, but in white ribbon. To make his plume, stitch or glue these upside down at the centre top of the helmet.

20. Fit the helmet on the doll, pinning it into position. Using a long darning needle and double thread, stitch to the head all the way round, close to the lower edge.

21. Pin wider gold braid around his face for the chin-strap, beginning and ending at the side of the helmet, just above the lower edge. Stitch into position. Make two 'buttons' as follows: coil a 10cm length of plaited black braid around to make a flat circle and stitch the edges together to hold in place. Finish off the end neatly, tucking it underneath. Stitch or glue one button over each end of the chin-strap.

CHAPTER 4

Magic Spells and Pumpkins

At last it was time for lunch. Baby Bear ate seven sandwiches, three sausage rolls, four tomatoes, two jam tarts, an apple and a slice of fruit cake.

'He's *always* hungry,' said Mother Bear, as he munched a big piece of pumpkin pie.

'I wish I had a pumpkin,' mused Baby Bear between mouthfuls, 'and I wish my Fairy Godmother would turn it into a golden coach for me to ride in.'

Father Bear burst out laughing and choked on his fruit cake. 'I can see you in a frilly pink ballgown with a diamond tiara,' he gasped. 'But your paws are much too big for those glass slippers.' And he roared with laughter again.

Baby Bear didn't like people laughing at him. So when he saw the brown butterfly, he jumped up and ran after it. But he tripped and fell into a bramble bush. Then he heard a soft voice and looked up to see a beautiful girl with hair the colour of honey. She wore a shabby patched dress and carried a broomstick. Baby Bear put his paw in her small hand and felt much happier.

'I'm Cinderella,' said the girl. 'My Fairy Godmother will make you better. She's looking for a pumpkin so that I can go to the ball.'

Baby Bear thought of all the pumpkin pie in his tummy and felt very guilty.

Cinderella's godmother was peering into a hollow tree. 'I've found a beautiful pumpkin,' she announced, 'but I can't find a small animal to turn into a coachman.'

She turned round and her worried expression cleared. '*Perfect!*' she exclaimed, beaming in delight at Baby Bear.

Suddenly Baby Bear changed his mind about fairy godmothers. He didn't fancy her waving her magic wand and turning him into something he didn't want to be, and then perhaps forgetting how to change him back. He looked wildly round for some way of escape and saw the butterfly.

'Goodbye!' he shouted as he dashed after it. 'Have a good time at the ball!'

He collapsed beside the picnic basket, exhausted. 'I'm hungry,' he puffed. 'Is there anything left to eat?'

Cinderella-in-Rags

Cinderella is a very attractive and appealing doll. Her long hair is caught back under a practical headscarf, but you could omit the scarf and allow it to frame her face and fall prettily round her shoulders. She is a lovely gift for a little girl, but also guaranteed to catch the customer's eye if you are planning to sell your dolls.

Much of Cinderella's appeal is in the pathos of the character. Emphasise the drab poverty of her costume by choosing all the fabrics in any sombre monotone. In this case, her dress, underskirt, apron and shoes are all in shades of brown, which tones with her honey-blonde hair. There is just one dramatic touch: the vibrantly contrasting scarf which she ties around her head.

If you enjoy planning exciting colour schemes, this is a wonderful design on which to let your artistic talents run riot. Shades of grey would be equally telling – perhaps with a fresh citrus-coloured headscarf in sharp lemon or tangy orange. Or, if you prefer more colour, imagine deep violet, grape, aubergine and purple, echoed in a brilliant shocking pink headscarf.

MATERIALS

Three 30cm (12in) squares of flesh-coloured felt
50g (2oz) honey-coloured double-knit yarn for hair
For other materials, see Basics 8, items 1–9 inclusive

40cm (½yd) medium-weight dark brown cotton-type fabric, 90 or 115cm (36 or 45in) wide, for dress
28cm (11in) medium-weight biscuit cotton-type fabric, 90 or 115cm (36 or 45in) wide, for underskirt
15cm (6in) square of flowered cotton-type fabric, for apron
30cm (12in) square (approximately) cotton handkerchief (or light-weight fabric), for headscarf
Scraps of toning fabric, for patches
50cm (⅝yd) light-weight cotton-type fabric, 90cm (36in) wide, for petticoat and pantalettes
12 × 20cm (4½ × 8in) dark brown felt, for shoes
30cm (12in) narrow white lace, for neckline
1m (1yd) dark brown ribbon, 1.5mm (1/16in) wide
20cm (¼yd) bias binding to match dress fabric
75cm (⅞yd) narrow round elastic
3 snap-fasteners
Matching threads
Clear adhesive

CINDERELLA: THE BASIC FIGURE

Follow the directions for the basic Fairytale Doll on page 19, using deep blue sequins for the eyes. For Cinderella's hair, see Basics 9.

CINDERELLA'S PETTICOAT AND PANTALETTES

1. Follow the directions given in Basics 10.

CINDERELLA'S BROWN DRESS, UNDERSKIRT AND APRON

2. Follow steps 6, 7 and 8 for Alice's dress (see page 50), but cut the skirt 25cm (10in) deep (see diagram). Then follow step 9 to the point where the skirt is joined to the bodice. Do *not* join the centre back seam.
3. Mark and gather the top edge of the underskirt exactly as you did the skirt, then pin behind the skirt gathers, side and top edges level, matching the marked points as before. Draw up the gathers to fit and stitch securely. *Note:* If you are worried that the dress will be too bulky around the waist, make the underskirt separately, with a waist elastic like the petticoat. Then you can draw it down so that the top edge falls just below the waistline of the dress.
4. Join the centre back seam of the skirt, leaving 8cm (3in) open at the top. Repeat for the underskirt. Turn under the centre back edges of the bodice as the broken line indicates and stitch.
5. Bind the neck edge neatly, stretching the binding as you sew it on.
6. Stitch snap-fasteners to the back opening at the neck, centre and waist. *Note:* Draw her undies down to just below waist level to avoid bulkiness, then pull the bodice as tightly as possible around the waist.
7. Turn under the raw lower edge of each sleeve, then fold under along the broken line and stitch the hem.
8. Turn under and stitch a 5cm (2in) hem around the skirt. Mark the lower edge of the skirt at each side (indicated with an X on the diagram). Using a double thread and making large (about 10–15mm/½in) stitches, gather each side of the skirt between the point marked with an X and the

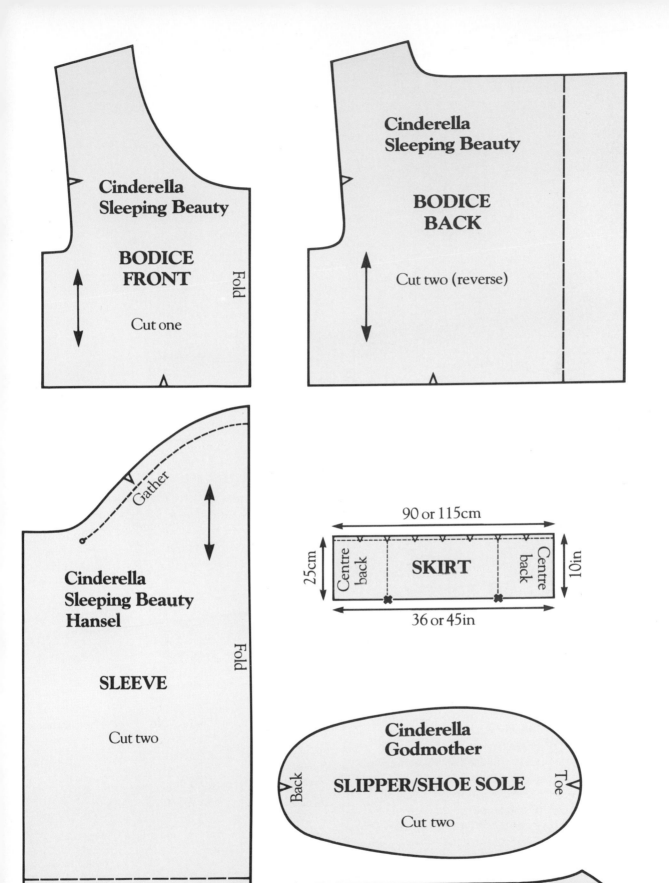

**Cinderella
Sleeping Beauty**

**BODICE
FRONT**

Cut one

Fold

**Cinderella
Sleeping Beauty**

**BODICE
BACK**

Cut two (reverse)

Gather

**Cinderella
Sleeping Beauty
Hansel**

SLEEVE

Cut two

Fold

90 or 115cm

25cm

Centre back

SKIRT

Centre back

10in

36 or 45in

**Cinderella
Godmother**

Back

SLIPPER/SHOE SOLE

Toe

Cut two

Back

**Cinderella
Godmother**

**SLIPPER/SHOE
UPPER**

Cut four (reverse two)

Toe

side seam of the bodice. Draw up tightly and secure.

9. Turn up and stitch a 2cm (¾in) hem around the underskirt.

10. Cut tiny patches in toning fabric and appliqué to the underskirt, as illustrated.

11. Gather the lace and pin evenly round the neck over the binding. Draw up to fit and stitch into place.

Make plaited braid (see Basics 6) from three 30cm (12in) lengths of ribbon, then glue over the gathered top edge of the lace.

12. Make a narrow hem around the sides and the lower edge of the apron. Turn under the top edge and gather. Draw up to measure 6cm (2¼in). With centres matching, pin over skirt gathers, immediately under the bodice. Distribute the gathers evenly and stitch into position.

CINDERELLA'S HEADSCARF

13. Fold the handkerchief diagonally and tie around the head, knotting the corners under the hair. (If you are using fabric, turn under a very narrow hem all round, or cut straight along the line of the fabric and draw a few threads from each raw edge.)

CINDERELLA'S SLIPPERS

14. Follow the directions given in Basics 10.

Cinderella's Fairy Godmother

In contrast to Cinderella's rags, her elegant Godmother would grace any occasion with her charming figure-fitting dress. The satin underskirt and ribbon trimmings pick up the colours of the flowers on the printed dress fabric, while deep lace frills trim the sleeves, the softly draped voile collar and her demure cap.

This is a doll for all ages, looking just as enchanting in a feminine bedroom or a nursery. Everybody needs a Fairy Godmother, so she would make a wonderful present for anyone from nine to ninety – as long as they believe in fairies!

MATERIALS

Three 30cm (12in) squares of flesh-coloured felt
50g (2oz) ball of mid-grey double-knit yarn for hair
For other materials see Basics 8, items 1–9 inclusive

50cm (½yd) medium-weight cotton-type fabric, 90cm (36in) wide, for dress
30cm (12in) lining satin, 90cm (36in) wide, for underskirt
60cm (⅝yd) light-weight cotton-type fabric, 90cm (36in) wide, for petticoat and pantalettes
25 × 35cm (10 × 14in) white voile (or organdie) for collar and cap
10 × 15cm (4 × 6in) matching coloured felt, and a 10cm (4in) square of beige felt, for shoes
1.7m (2yd) white lace, 30mm (1¼in) deep, for collar, sleeves and cap
1m (36in) lace, 10mm (⅜in) deep, to match underskirt
80cm (⅞yd) Colonial Rose single-face satin ribbon, 9mm (⅜in) wide, for roses and bows
15cm (6in) Colonial Rose single-face satin ribbon, 6mm (¼in) wide, for neck rose (or use 9mm/⅜in)
65cm (¾yd) bias binding to match dress fabric
30cm (12in) white bias binding
2 tear-drop pearl beads, about 12mm (½in) deep
2 tiny glass or pearl beads (to anchor above)
70cm (¾yd) narrow round elastic
3 snap-fasteners
Matching threads

FAIRY GODMOTHER: THE BASIC FIGURE

Follow the directions for the basic Fairytale Doll on page 19. Use blue sequins for the eyes and omit the nose. For the Fairy Godmother's hair, see Basics 9.

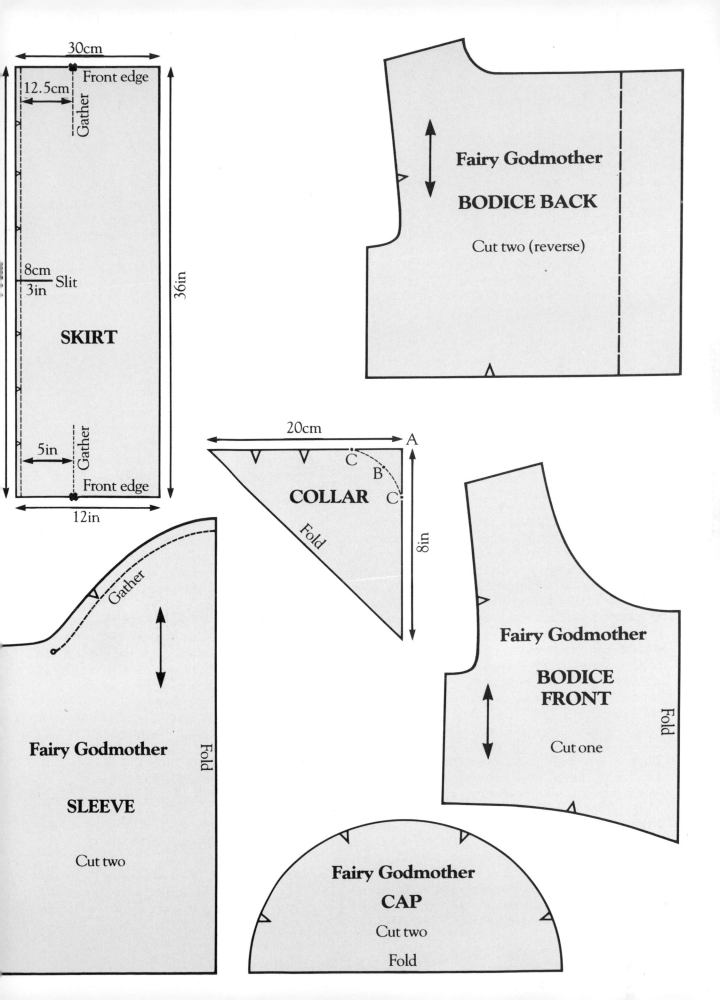

SKIRT

30cm

12.5cm

Gather

Front edge

8cm
3in — Slit

36in

5in

Gather

Front edge

12in

Fairy Godmother

BODICE BACK

Cut two (reverse)

COLLAR

20cm

A

C
B
C

Fold

8in

Fairy Godmother

BODICE FRONT

Cut one

Fold

Gather

Fairy Godmother

SLEEVE

Cut two

Fold

Fairy Godmother

CAP

Cut two

Fold

FAIRY GODMOTHER'S PETTICOAT AND PANTALETTES

1. Follow the directions given in Basics 10.

FAIRY GODMOTHER'S ROSE-TRIMMED GOWN AND UNDERSKIRT

2. Make up the 30 × 90cm (12 × 36in) satin as directed for the petticoat, but turn up the hem so that it almost touches the ground, and then trim the lower edge with matching lace.

3. Follow steps 6, 7 and 8 for Alice's dress (see page 50), but cut the skirt 30cm (12in) deep (see diagram). At the end of step 8, turn up and tack a narrow hem around the lower edge of the bodice.

4. Turn under each side edge of the skirt and make a 1.5cm (⅝in) hem; these will be the centre front edges (see diagram). Make an 8cm (3in) deep slit for the centre back opening, as indicated. Bind the raw edges, turning the whole width of the binding over to the wrong side, then catch together a pleat at the base to strengthen and neaten. Mark each half of the top edge equally into four, then gather both sides to within 2cm (¾in) of back opening.

5. Pin the wrong side of the bodice over the right side of the skirt gathers, matching the marked points to the notches and side seams of the bodice. The front edges of the skirt should meet under the centre front point of the bodice, and each bound edge of the back opening should be level with the broken line on the bodice pattern. Draw up the gathers distributing them evenly between the pins, then stitch the edge of the bodice to the skirt.

6. Mark each front edge of the skirt 12.5cm (5in) below the point of the bodice (marked with an X on the diagram). Beginning at the marked point, gather across each side in a horizontal line, as indicated, for 15cm (6in). Draw up tightly and secure. Make a rose (see Basics 6) for each side from 20–5cm (8–9in) of 9mm (⅜in) ribbon, and stitch over the gathers as illustrated.

7. Turn under the back edges of the bodice along the broken line and stitch.

8. Bind the raw edges of the neck (stretch the binding as you sew it on) and sleeves.

9. For each wrist frill, join the cut edges of an 18–20cm (7–8in) length of white lace, then gather about 3mm (⅛in) below the top edge. Pin gathers evenly over the sleeve binding, then draw up to fit and stitch. Make two butterfly bows from 10cm (4in) of 9mm (⅜in) ribbon (see Basics 6, page 12: mark points B 2.5cm (1in) from point A). Stitch one just above the lace on each sleeve, as illustrated.

10. Fit the dress on the doll, over the underskirt. Mark the centre back opening, then stitch snap-fasteners at the top, centre and waist. Turn up the hem of the skirt and stitch.

11. To hold the underskirt in the correct position, catch the centre front point of the bodice to the top of the underskirt, and catch the underside of the back opening to the centre back.

12. Cut a 20cm (8in) square of voile for the collar. Fold in half diagonally and pin, as shown in the diagram. Mark point B 2.5cm (1in) from point A, and points C 5cm (2in) from point A. Cut off the corner as indicated by the broken line. Stitch close to the edge, leaving 5cm (2in) open between the notches to turn. Clip corners and turn to the right side. Turn in the raw edges and pin, then top stitch all round, close to the edge (but not along the fold).

Gather 45cm (½yd) white lace 3mm (⅛in) below the top edge. Mark both the lace and the edge of the collar equally into eight, then pin the gathering line over the top stitching so that the remaining lace overlaps the edge of the collar. Draw up the gathers evenly between the pins and stitch into place. Gather each cut edge and draw up tightly.

Make a rose from the 6mm (¼in) ribbon and stitch to the centre front of the neck binding. Drape the collar around the neck as illustrated and catch the front points to the bodice to hold in position.

13. Cut the cap twice in voile. Tack the two pieces together around the edge to keep them absolutely flat, then bind the edge. Stitch 50cm (½yd) gathered lace around the edge as described for the collar.

Stitch the centre of a 30cm (12in) length of lace underneath the centre back edge of the cap to hang down for the streamers. Then make a ribbon bow as for the sleeves, but mark points B 3cm (1¼in) from point A. Stitch over top of streamers.

14. Stitch a pearl bead just under the hair at each side of the face for her earrings, anchoring in place with a tiny bead.

FAIRY GODMOTHER'S SHOES

15. Follow directions given in Basics 10.

CHAPTER 5

Wicked Witches and Hungry Wolves

An overgrown path led through a very dense part of the forest and twigs kept getting caught in Baby Bear's fur.

He asked his mother for a lollipop, but she offered him an apple.

'I want a lollipop,' he grumbled. 'I could eat a *house* full of lollipops.' Then he had an idea. 'Perhaps we'll find a cottage all made of gingerbread and sweets – like the one in the story.'

'Of course not!' laughed his father. 'And remember, a wicked witch lived in that particular cottage, so if you tried to eat *those* sweets, you might find the witch eating *you* instead!'

Baby Bear shivered. He looked around uneasily and saw the butterfly hovering on a tree-stump. Then he heard footsteps. It was a little girl in a red cape, the hood drawn over her dark hair.

'You're Little Red Riding Hood!' he exclaimed, clapping his paws in delight.

'I'm going to see my grandmother,' she replied. 'Would you like to come too?'

'No thank you,' Baby Bear refused politely. 'Your grandmother might be a wolf in disguise.'

'What a ridiculous idea!' she giggled. 'You *are* a silly little bear.'

Then Baby Bear spotted a boy and a girl knocking at the door of a pretty cottage. He was sure they were Hansel and Gretel.

He ran forward shouting: 'You mustn't go in!' But they simply knocked again.

'A wicked witch lives there,' he said. 'She'll put you in a cage and eat you!'

'Nonsense!' laughed the boy. 'We're having tea with a kind old lady. You can come too. And bring your friend.' Red Riding Hood smiled eagerly.

They took Baby Bear's paws and drew him towards the cottage. 'I'm not going in'!, he shouted wildly and managed to wriggle free. He looked in desperation for the butterfly. It flew down from the cottage roof and Baby Bear ran after it. The three children watched him go, laughing at his strange warnings and odd behaviour.

'You look pale, dear,' said his mother. 'Would you like a slice of gingerbread?'

'No thank you,' said Baby Bear, 'I think I'll have an apple.'

Hansel

Although Hansel and Gretel are inseparable in fiction, there is no reason why they should be in the nursery. It is a sad fact that even in these days of equal rights, boys are badly neglected by doll designers; among all those charming moppets with frilly petticoats and ringlets, there are few characters which are suitable for small boys. But as every little girl knows, there's nothing more comforting than your favourite doll to cuddle when you're tucked up in bed and feeling all alone, or when you wake up in the night and you need someone to talk to.

So why *should* boys have to rely on teddy bears or blue bunnies for companionship? If you want to head the campaign – especially if you are selling your work – Hansel is just the kind of youngster who will appeal to children and adults alike. There's just a hint of mischief in his wide-eyed expression of innocence – and every mother will long to take a comb to that tousled mop of hair!

MATERIALS

Three 30cm (12in) squares of flesh-coloured felt
50g (2oz) ball of honey-coloured double-knit yarn for hair (use the remainder for Gretel)
For other materials, see Basics 8, items 1–9 inclusive

16 × 65cm (6½ × 25in) yellow cotton-type fabric, for shirt
Checked cotton handkerchief (or light-weight fabric), for neckerchief (at least 20cm (8in) square)
22 × 35cm (8½ × 14in) olive-green felt, for breeches
11 × 24cm (4½ × 9½in) black felt, for waistcoat (vest)
15 × 20cm (6 × 8in) dark brown felt, for boots
4cm (1½in) white guipure lace daisies (about 1cm (⅜in) in diameter), or similar trim
15cm (6in) bias binding to match shirt
25cm (10in) bias binding to match breeches
25cm (¼yd) narrow round elastic
5 snap-fasteners
Matching threads

HANSEL: THE BASIC FIGURE

Follow the directions for the basic Fairytale Doll on page 19, using green sequins for the eyes. For Hansel's hair, see Basics 9.

HANSEL'S SHIRT

1. Use the pattern pieces for the back and front of the Mad Hatter's shirt; use the pattern for Cinderella's sleeve. Then follow steps 1–4 for the Mad Hatter's shirt (page 53). (*Note*: When setting in the sleeves (step 3) match the sides and centre but ignore the notches, then use the gathers to ease in.)
2. Turn under the raw lower edge of each sleeve, then turn under along the broken line and stitch hem.
3. Bind the neck neatly. Stitch snap-fasteners inside the front opening at the neck, centre and waist.

HANSEL'S GREEN FELT BREECHES

4. Follow the directions given in Basics 10.

HANSEL'S WAISTCOAT (VEST)

5. Use the pattern pieces for the Mad Hatter's waistcoat (page 56). Make up as directed: steps 13–15.
6. Stitch lace trim down centre front, as illustrated.

HANSEL'S NECKERCHIEF

7. Cut a 20cm (8in) square from a handkerchief or fabric. Turn the raw edges under and make a very narrow hem, or cut straight along the line of the fabric and draw a few threads. Fold diagonally and tie around the neck, catching corners together at the front.

HANSEL'S BOOTS

8. Cut the upper and sole twice each in brown felt.
9. For each boot, fold the upper in half (as shown in the pattern) and oversew between the toe and notch. Pin the lower edge to the sole, matching seams to notches, then oversew. Turn to the right side.

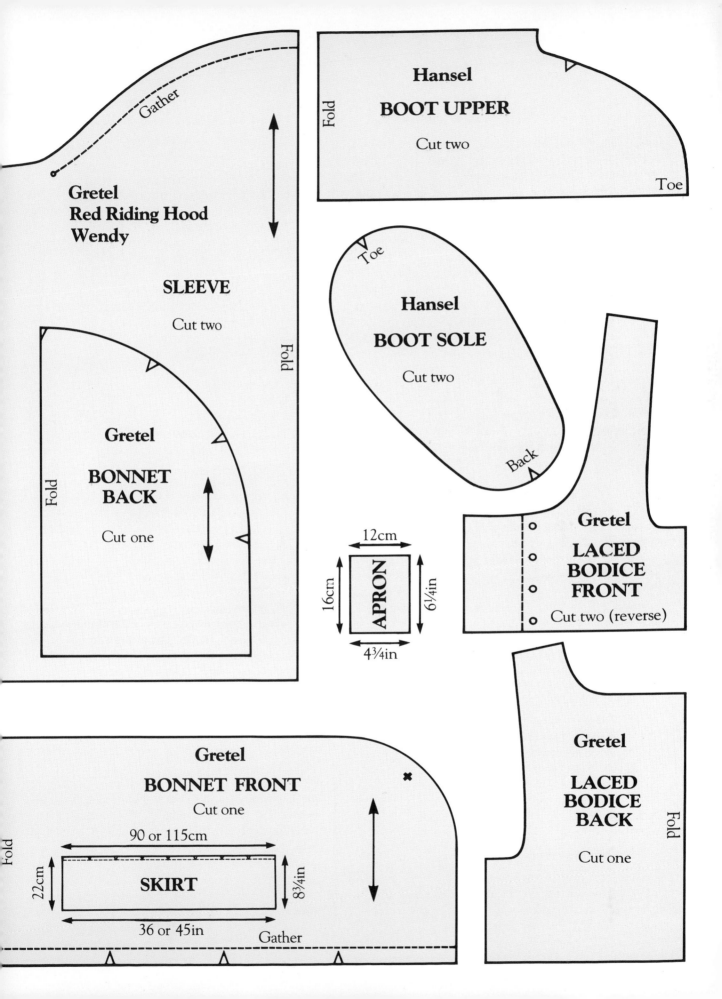

Gather

**Gretel
Red Riding Hood
Wendy**

SLEEVE

Cut two

Fold

**Hansel
BOOT UPPER**

Cut two

Fold

Toe

Toe

**Hansel
BOOT SOLE**

Cut two

Back

**Gretel
BONNET
BACK**

Cut one

Fold

12cm

APRON

16cm

6¼in

4¾in

**Gretel
LACED
BODICE
FRONT**

Cut two (reverse)

**Gretel
BONNET FRONT**

Cut one

Fold

90 or 115cm

22cm

SKIRT

8¾in

36 or 45in

Gather

**Gretel
LACED
BODICE
BACK**

Cut one

Fold

Gretel

Although she is the perfect partner for Hansel, Gretel can stand on her own as the kind of traditional doll which little girls love to love. Her pretty peasant-style outfit gives you scope to plan an artistic combination of fabrics, accentuated by crisp touches of black and white.

Gretel is an ideal subject if you intend to sell your work. The joined blouse-and-skirt dress is quick to make, and the variety of fabrics and colours means that no two dolls need be exactly alike. Make some with dark hair too, and choose other hairstyles. Give her a fringe or braid her hair in plaits or sweep it up in a top-knot. Turn to the hairstyles section (see Basics 9) for inspiration.

MATERIALS

Three 30cm (12in) squares of flesh-coloured felt
50g (2oz) ball of honey-coloured double-knit yarn for hair (use the remainder for Hansel)
For other materials, see Basics 8, items 1–9 inclusive

30cm (12in) medium-weight flower-patterned white cotton-type fabric, 90cm (36in) wide, for the blouse and pantalettes
22cm (8¾in) medium-weight olive-green cotton-type fabric, 90 or 115cm (36 or 45in) wide, for the skirt
23cm (¼yd) medium-weight yellow cotton-type fabric, 90cm (36in) wide, for the petticoat
20 × 40cm (8 × 16in) white spotted voile (dotted Swiss), or similar fabric, for the bonnet and apron
20cm (8in) square black felt for the bodice and shoes
1.1m (1¼yd) white guipure lace daisies (about 1cm (⅜in) diameter), or similar trim
50cm (½yd) white satin ribbon, 3mm (⅛in) wide
30cm (12in) black satin ribbon, 1.5mm (¹⁄₁₆in) wide
50cm (⅝yd) white bias binding (or to match blouse)
1m (1⅛yd) narrow round elastic
3 snap-fasteners
Matching threads
Clear adhesive

GRETEL: THE BASIC FIGURE

Follow the directions for the basic Fairytale Doll on page 19, using green sequins for the eyes. For Gretel's hair, see Basics 9.

GRETEL'S PETTICOAT AND PANTALETTES

1. Using yellow fabric for the petticoat, and flower-patterned white fabric for the pantalettes, follow the directions in Basics 10.

GRETEL'S BLOUSE-AND-SKIRT STYLE DRESS AND APRON

2. Use the Gretel sleeve pattern with the bodice front and back for Alice's dress (page 51). Cut the bodice front once, and the back and sleeve twice each, in flowered fabric.

Then cut a strip 22cm (8¾in) deep, right across the width of the green fabric, for the skirt (see diagram).

Cut the apron (see diagram) and the bonnet front and back once each, in spotted voile.
3. Follow the directions for Alice's dress, steps 7–11 inclusive.
4. Stitch lace daisy trimming over neck binding.
5. Bind the raw lower edge of each sleeve, then thread elastic through and draw up to fit wrist.
6. Turn up and stitch a 2cm (¾in) hem around the lower edge of the skirt.
7. Turn under a very narrow hem along the side and lower edges of the apron, then turn under the top edge and gather: draw up to measure 7cm (2¾in) and secure. Stitch lace daisies all around the side and lower edges.
8. With centres matching, pin top edge of the apron level with top edge of skirt. Distributing gathers evenly, stitch neatly into place.
9. Fit the dress on the doll and turn up the hem of petticoat so that it shows 2.5cm (1in) below the skirt.

GRETEL'S BLACK FELT, LACED BODICE

10. Cut the back once and the front twice in black felt. Oversew the shoulder and side seams, to join.
11. Fold under the centre front edges as broken line, and glue. Then make tiny holes (with a punch, if you have one) as indicated on the pattern. Fit bodice on doll and thread black ribbon through the holes as diagram, tying a bow at the bottom.

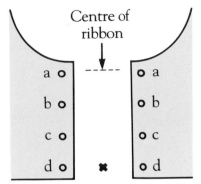

Centre of
ribbon

Ends down through a: cross ribbon
Ends up through b: cross ribbon
Repeat through c & d
Tie at X

GRETEL'S LACE-EDGED BONNET

12. Gather along the back edge of the front piece. Pin round the curved edge of the back, matching side-edges and notches. Draw up to fit and stitch.
13. Turn under the raw edge and make a very narrow hem. Sew daisies all round, slightly overlapping the edge.
14. Cut the white ribbon in half for bonnet strings. Stitch top ends inside the front corners at the point marked with an X.

GRETEL'S SHOES

15. Follow the directions in Basics 10, using the patterns for Alice's shoes.

Little Red Riding Hood

This eye-catching doll is an ideal choice if you are keen to make a profit. It is designed for the sewing-machine, with lots of straight seams, minimal trimming and hardly any handwork.

The deep hem on the petticoat makes Red Riding Hood's flirty skirt stand out prettily, which in turn shows off her long shapely legs in their alluring black stockings. Scarlet is an exciting colour to work with and is even more dramatic when teamed with black. Have fun with fabrics too. This version plays around with polka dots and checks to achieve a carefully co-ordinated outfit.

MATERIALS

Two 30cm (12in) squares of flesh felt
One 30cm (12in) square of black felt, for legs and shoes
50g (2oz) ball dark brown double-knit yarn, for hair
For other materials, see Basics 8, items 1–9 inclusive

50cm (⅝yd) medium-weight cotton-type scarlet fabric with black polka-dot, 90cm (36in) wide, for cape
20cm (8in) medium-weight cotton-type scarlet-and-black check fabric, 90cm (36in) wide, for skirt
40cm (15in) light-weight cotton-type white fabric with red polka-dot, 90cm (36in) wide, for blouse and undies
10 × 15cm (4 × 6in) scarlet felt for shoes
1.3m (1⅜yd) lace, about 10mm (⅜in) deep, to trim petticoat and panties

60cm (¾yd) black single-face satin ribbon, 6mm (¼in) wide
50cm (⅝yd) bias binding to tone with blouse
1m (1⅛yd) narrow round elastic
3 snap-fasteners
Matching threads

LITTLE RED RIDING HOOD: THE BASIC FIGURE

Follow the directions for the basic Fairytale Doll on page 19, but cut the legs and soles in black felt. Use dark blue sequins for the eyes. For Red Riding Hood's hair, see Basics 9.

RED RIDING HOOD'S PETTICOAT AND PANTIES

1. Follow the directions in Basics 10.

RED RIDING HOOD'S BLOUSE-AND-SKIRT STYLE DRESS

2. Use the Gretel sleeve pattern with the bodice front and back for Alice's dress (page 51). Cut the bodice front once, and the back and sleeve twice each, in spotted white fabric.

Cut a strip 18cm (7in) deep, right across the width of the check fabric, for the skirt (see diagram).

3. Follow the directions for Alice's dress, steps 7–11 inclusive.

4. Bind the raw lower edge of each sleeve, then thread elastic through and draw up to fit wrist.

5. Turn up and stitch a 2cm (¾in) hem around the lower edge of the skirt.

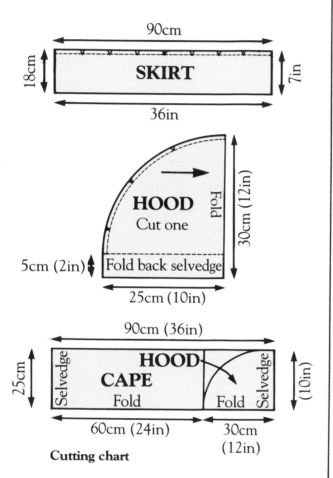

Cutting chart

RED RIDING HOOD'S LINED CAPE

6. Make the hood pattern following the diagram, then fold your fabric in half widthways and cut the hood and cape as indicated on the cutting chart.

7. With the wrong side inside, fold the selvedge back 5cm (2in) to form the front edge of the hood. Stitch, close to the selvedge, then make a second line of stitches, 5mm (¼in) in front of the first, forming a channel. Trim the side edges level.

Gather the curved edge, then mark into eight.

8. With the right side inside, fold the cape in half widthways (as shown in the cutting diagram) and stitch the side edges to 1.5cm (⅝in) from the top. Turn to the right side, then tack and press these seams to form crisp edges for the front of the cape.

9. Mark the top edge equally into eight. With right sides together and beginning and ending 2cm (¾in) from the front edges, pin lower edge of hood to top edge of cape, matching marked points. Draw up gathers to fit, distributing them evenly, and stitch. Turn under the raw top edge inside the cape and slip stitch over gathers inside the hood. Oversew top edges of cape at each end beyond the hood.

10. Make a line of stitches 1cm (⅜in) below the top edge of the cape, to form a channel. Press the whole garment.

11. Thread elastic through hood and draw up to fit around head, then secure at each end.

12. Thread ribbon through neck and draw up to fit. Tie in a bow.

RED RIDING HOOD'S SCARLET SHOES

13. With scarlet felt for the uppers, and black for the soles, follow the directions in Basics 10, using the patterns for Alice's shoes.

CHAPTER 6

Flight to Neverland

Now they were on their way back. Picnics were such exciting things, thought Baby Bear, but it was a greaty pity they involved so much walking. He gazed dreamily at Mother Bear's basket.

'Are we going to stop for tea soon?' he ventured in a small voice.

'Do you never think of anything else but food?' exploded his father. 'I have never, never come across such a greedy bear. You are never, never satisfied.'

'Never, never, never,' repeated Baby Bear to himself. 'Just like Neverland!'

The butterfly was resting on a twig. As he watched it flutter off, he suddenly realised that his feet weren't touching the ground any more – he was flying. He glanced round and saw Father Bear gliding through the clouds behind him.

They flew for a long time until Baby Bear looked down and saw a boy dressed in green waving to them. He was joined by a girl who was wearing a frilly nightgown. The bears landed at their feet with a bump.

Peter Pan and Wendy welcomed them to the Neverland and Wendy made a great fuss of Baby Bear. He was just about to mention that flying seemed to make him very hungry, when there was a loud ticking noise, and he saw a big crocodile coming towards them from the river. And he remembered how, in the story, the crocodile had swallowed an alarm clock.

Then he heard rough voices shouting and turned to see a bearded sea-captain, followed by a group of blood-thirsty pirates, their knives flashing in the sun.

'It's Captain Hook!' yelled Peter and, grabbing Wendy's hand, they flew off.

Baby Bear was terrified. He was about to be murdered by pirates – if he wasn't eaten by a crocodile first. He looked in vain for the butterfly. Then suddenly his feet left the ground and he was in the air. Something was tickling his head: it was the butterfly.

'Now then, my boy,' grunted Father Bear when they had landed safely. 'You are never, never to fly off like that again.'

'No,' replied Baby Bear in a very small voice, 'I've never been there before, and I'm never going there again!'

Peter Pan

Peter Pan is especially suitable for little boys. Also, there's very little work in making the doll and only a short list of materials is required – all of which makes it ideal for quick production if you are selling your work. The most time-consuming operation is the cut-out leaves, but these may be omitted altogether. If so, make the legs in a darker green, to emphasise the pointed edge of the tunic.

If you are going to make the outfit as it is illustrated here, choose the most autumnal shades you can find to harmonise with a leafy olive-green felt for the main garments, then top it all with a cheeky bright green cap.

MATERIALS

Two 30cm (12in) squares of flesh felt
50g (2oz) ball of reddish-brown double-knit yarn, for hair
For other materials, see Basics 8, items 1–9 inclusive

20 × 60cm (8 × 24in) mid-olive-green felt, for main outfit (including legs)
23cm (9in) square of bright-green felt, for hat
15cm (6in) square of golden-brown felt, for yoke
15cm (6in) square of gold felt, for leaves
10cm (4in) square of mid-brown felt, for leaves
15 × 20cm (6 × 8in) russet brown felt, for leaves
15 × 20cm (6 × 8in) russet brown felt, for shoes
4 snap-fasteners
Matching threads
Clear adhesive

PETER PAN: THE BASIC FIGURE

Follow the directions for the basic Fairytale Doll on page 19, but trace the patterns for the body back and front in two separate halves. Divide the pattern pieces as indicated, adding 3mm (⅛in) to each edge for joining. Cut the upper body in flesh felt, and the lower part in olive green. Oversew together and make up in the usual way, cutting the legs and soles in green also. Use green sequins for the eyes. For Peter Pan's hair, see Basics 9.

PETER'S TUNIC

1. Cut the front once, and the back and sleeve twice each, in olive-green felt. Cut the yoke in golden-brown felt. Cut 22 leaves in gold felt and 10 in mid-brown.
2. Join the front to the back pieces at the shoulders, then set in the sleeves, matching the side edges and the centre to the shoulder seam. Join the side and sleeve seams. Turn under and stitch the edges of the centre back opening, as indicated by the broken line.
3. Stitch snap-fasteners to centre back opening as shown by the circles on the pattern (fit the tunic on the doll to determine overlap).
4. Following the illustration, glue gold leaves *behind* the lower edge of the tunic, between each V, so that the tips of the leaves are about 6mm (¼in) lower than the points of the Vs (spread glue on leaf as indicated by the wavy line on the pattern). Then glue brown leaves behind and between the gold ones, so that they fall about 12mm (½in) below the point of each V.
5. Glue gold leaves between the points of the yoke in the same way. Pin the yoke to the tunic, matching the neck edges. Stitch the back neck and centre back edges of the yoke to the tunic as indicated by the broken lines on the pattern, but only tack it at the front. Catch everything securely together across the base of the centre front slit (between the points marked with an X) with a few stitches in matching thread. Then turn back the top corners of the centre front opening as illustrated and catch down neatly.

PETER'S POINTED CAP

6. Cut the pattern piece four times in bright green felt.
7. Join the side edges of the four sections to form a conical hat shape and turn to the right side.
8. Fit the hat on the doll and catch to the head at the base of each seam.

PETER'S RUSSET SHOES

9. Cut the upper and sole twice each in russet felt.
10. To make each shoe, fold the upper in half, wrong side inside. Oversew the front edges, then turn to the wrong side. Fit the upper around the edge of the sole, matching the centre back and front seam to notches, then stitch together. Turn to the right side.

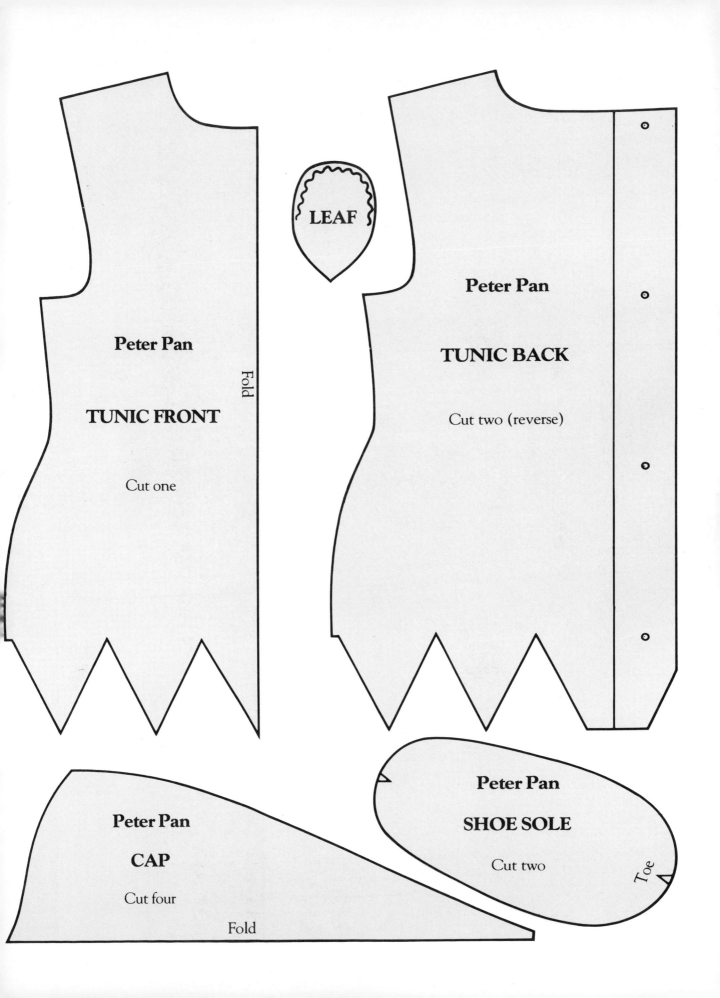

LEAF

Peter Pan

TUNIC FRONT

Cut one

Fold

Peter Pan

TUNIC BACK

Cut two (reverse)

Peter Pan

CAP

Cut four

Fold

Peter Pan

SHOE SOLE

Cut two

Toe

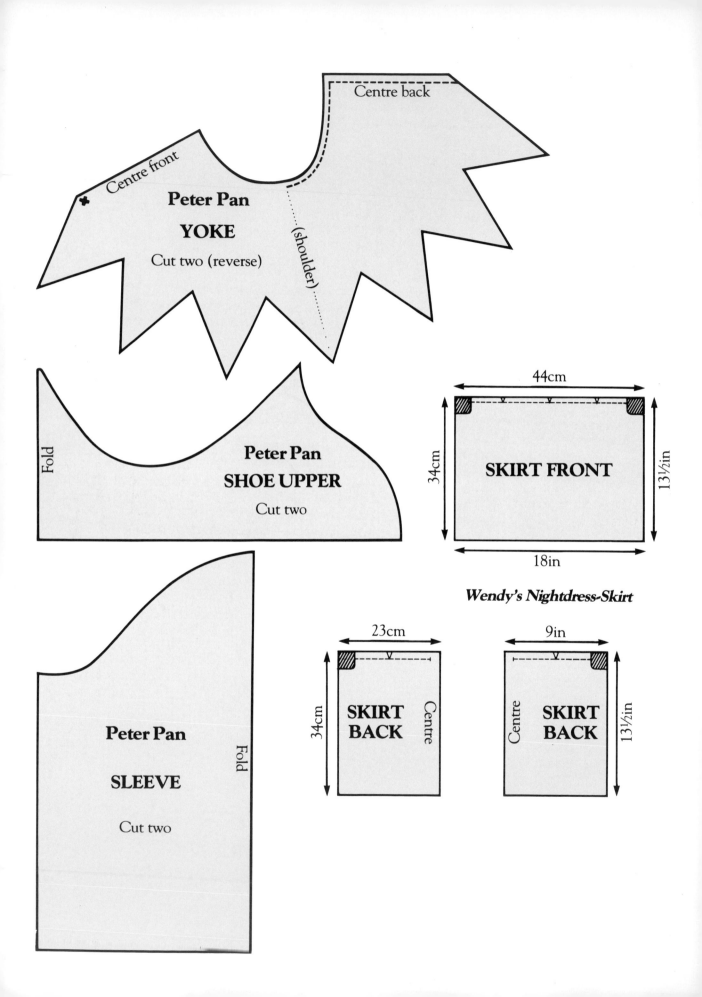

Peter Pan

YOKE

Cut two (reverse)

Centre front

Centre back

(shoulder)

Peter Pan

SHOE UPPER

Cut two

Fold

44cm

13½in

SKIRT FRONT

34cm

18in

Wendy's Nightdress-Skirt

Peter Pan

SLEEVE

Cut two

Fold

23cm

34cm

SKIRT BACK

Centre

9in

13½in

Centre

SKIRT BACK

Wendy

When Peter Pan persuaded Wendy Darling to fly with him to the Neverland, he was unwittingly making her demure nightie one of the best-known garments in fiction!

This charming doll personifies the gentle, affectionate character which J. M. Barrie created in *Peter Pan and Wendy* – the warm-hearted girl who left her comfortable home to care for Peter and mother his lost boys. If you can manage to separate her from her beloved Peter, Wendy is the perfect doll to charm a little girl at bed-time – and, of course, to sit on her bed, smiling prettily, all day.

This design lends itself to adaptation, and one useful idea is a Wendy nightdress case. First make the doll, omitting the legs. Then make a 'petticoat' from a firm medium-weight fabric, joining the lower edges to form a bag which is large enough to hold the owner's nightwear. Leave an opening in the centre back seam which is large enough to get the contents in and out easily (this can be left open, or closed either with Velcro or a zip fastener). Stitch the gathered top edge of the petticoat-bag securely around the waist, then make the nightdress as instructed, but cut the skirt much longer so that the bag is completely covered.

MATERIALS

Three 30cm (12in) squares of flesh-coloured felt
50g (2oz) ball of dark brown double-knit yarn, for hair
For other materials, see Basics 8, items 1–9 inclusive

55cm (⅝yd) medium-weight printed cotton-type
   fabric, 90cm (36in) wide
50cm (½yd) broderie anglaise (eyelet embroidery),
   about 5cm (2in) deep
1.5m (1⅝yd) white lace, about 10mm (⅜in) deep
20cm (8in) bias binding to match fabric
25cm (¼yd) narrow round elastic
2 snap-fasteners
Matching threads

WENDY: THE BASIC FIGURE

Follow the directions for the basic Fairytale Doll on page 19, using blue sequins for the eyes. For Wendy's hair, see Basics 9.

WENDY'S NIGHTDRESS

1. Cut a 34cm (13½in) deep strip right across the width of the fabric for the skirt. Divide this into two pieces 23cm (9in) wide for the back, and one piece 44cm (18in) wide for the front. Turn to the directions for Clara's party frock (page 65) and cut armholes in the skirt pieces as instructed (step 6).
2. Using the bodice patterns for Clara's party frock, cut the front once and the back twice. Cut the sleeve pattern for Gretel's blouse (page 89) twice.
3. Follow the directions for Clara's party frock, steps 7–13 inclusive, using alternative lace (as above) to trim the sleeves and form a tiny stand-up collar.
4. Fit the nightdress on the doll and turn up the hem. Stitch, then trim with a band of lace, over the stitching line.
5. Run a gathering thread about 3.5cm (1⅜in) above the lower edge of the broderie anglaise. Fold it along this line, turning the raw top edge over to the wrong side, and tack just below the fold. Pin the broderie anglaise evenly around the yoke, beginning and ending at the centre back opening. Keep it level with the top of the sleeve at the end of the shoulder seams, dropping the curve to about 1.5cm (⅝in) at the centre front. Draw up the gathers and stitch neatly into place.

CHAPTER 7

The Enchanted Castle

They were taking a short cut and the narrow path was overgrown with ivy. Baby Bear pretended that he was in an enchanted castle, rescuing a sleeping princess. When he kissed her, she would wake up and fall in love with him and they would get married and live happily ever after.

The butterfly fluttered lazily past him, towards the ivy-clad stone walls of a castle – which he was sure hadn't been there a moment ago. One wall had crumbled away and Baby Bear could see a handsome young man looking down at a beautiful girl, who lay on a big bed.

Suddenly the young man saw Baby Bear.

'And who might you be?' he demanded.

'I'm Baby Bear. And my Daddy and Mummy are Mr and Mrs Bear,' he told the young man proudly.

'Well, I'm Prince Florimund. I've just kissed the Sleeping Beauty and now she's about to fall in love with me. So *you* must be in the wrong story.'

'Yes I am,' admitted Baby Bear cheerfully, 'but I like this story and I want to see you kiss her again.'

The handsome prince strode towards him with a dark frown. He spoke very slowly and firmly. 'I have waited a hundred years for this moment,' he said, 'and I'm *not* going to have it ruined by a nosy little bear peeping through the keyhole.'

'But there isn't a keyhole to peep through!' protested Baby Bear.

'No,' agreed the Prince, 'but if there was one, you are the kind of bear who would peep through it.'

Baby Bear felt this was most unfair – though, of course, it was perfectly true.

'If you don't disappear immediately,' Prince Florimund threatened, 'I will personally arrange for the Bad Fairy to prick your paw with her spinning wheel . . . and you will go to sleep for a hundred years.'

As Baby Bear ran through the bushes, he heard the Prince shouting. 'And don't expect *me* to come and wake you up!'

Mother Bear said she thought he looked tired. 'Would you like to stop and have a little sleep?' she asked.

'No!' puffed Baby Bear anxiously. 'I'd rather wait until we get home!'

The Sleeping Beauty

Awakening to the Prince's kiss, the Sleeping Beauty opens her eyes, and becomes the gorgeous doll every little girl dreams of owning. And for little girls who grew up too soon, the Sleeping Beauty could add her graceful royal presence to a dainty grown-up bedroom.

Although she looks so glamorous, Sleeping Beauty's dress is in fact very simple. You can see Cinderella wearing the ragged version on page 78. The secret lies in the fabric – shimmering white satin scattered with tiny rosebuds – and the trimmings of ribbons, lace and pearls. Satin is not easy to work with on this scale because tiny pattern pieces tend to fray, but this is overcome by using the thinnest iron-on interlining. This stiffens the fabric a little, so choose a very soft satin. The rosebud print used here is from the bridal department.

MATERIALS

Three 30cm (12in) squares of flesh-coloured felt
50g (2oz) ball of russet-coloured double-knit yarn, for hair
For other materials, see Basics 8, items 1–9 inclusive

50cm (½yd) printed satin, 90 or 115cm (36 or 45in) wide
60cm (⅝yd) light-weight cotton-type fabric, 90cm (36in) wide, for petticoat and pantalettes
10 × 15cm (4 × 6in) pink felt, and a 10cm (4in) square of beige felt, for shoes
15 × 60cm (6 × 24in) lightest-weight iron-on interlining
1.6m (1¾yd) white lace, 20mm (¾in) deep, to trim neck and sleeves
1.1 or 1.35m (1¼ or 1½yd)* very narrow white lace to trim hem, etc (*according to fabric width)
2.7m (3yd) cream lace, 15mm (⅝in) deep, to trim undies
50cm (⅝yd) Colonial Rose feather-edge satin ribbon, 9mm (⅜in) wide, to trim waist and sleeves
45cm (½yd) Colonial Rose single-face satin ribbon, 6mm (¼in) wide
15cm (6in) Colonial Rose satin ribbon, 3mm (⅛in) wide
1m (1yd) Willow Green satin ribbon, 1.5mm (1/16in) wide
2.1m (2⅜yd) white satin ribbon, 1.5mm (1/16in) wide

1m (1yd) each pink and white tiny pearl bead trimming
Tiny pink and white artificial flowers, for hair
20cm (¼yd) white bias binding
50cm (½yd) narrow round elastic
3 snap-fasteners
Matching threads
Clear adhesive

THE SLEEPING BEAUTY: THE BASIC FIGURE

Follow the directions for the basic Fairytale Doll on page 19, using blue sequins for the eyes. For Sleeping Beauty's hair, see Basics 9.

SLEEPING BEAUTY'S PETTICOAT AND PANTALETTES

1. Follow the directions in Basics 10.

SLEEPING BEAUTY'S ROSEBUD DRESS

2. Cut a strip 30cm (12in) deep, right across the width of the fabric, for the skirt (see diagram below).

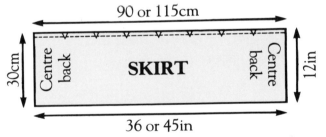

3. Use the bodice front and back and the sleeve patterns for Cinderella's dress (page 81). Back satin with iron-on interlining, then cut the bodice front once and the back and sleeve twice each.
4. Follow steps 7–11 for Alice's dress (page 50).
5. Turn under the lower edge of each sleeve as indicated by the broken line, and hem.
6. Gather 30cm (12in) of the wider white lace, then stitch around the neck, level with the outer (lower) edge of the binding, distributing the gathers evenly.

Gather a similar piece and stitch this just below the inner (upper) edge of the binding, to fall over the previous frill.

Make plaited braid (see Basics 6) from three 30cm (12in) lengths of white ribbon, then glue over the gathered top edge of the lace.

7. Gather 23cm (9in) of the same lace and stitch evenly around the sleeve, close to the edge. Stitch a similar piece 5mm (¼in) above.

Plait three 20cm (8in) lengths of white ribbon and glue over the top gathers.

Make two butterfly bows from 12cm (5in) feather-edge ribbon (see Basics 6: mark points B 3cm (1¼in) from A). Stitch one just above the lace on each sleeve, as illustrated.

8. Fit feather-edge ribbon sash around waist, stitching ends at centre back and catching at each side.

Make a rose (see Basics 6) from 15cm (6in), 6mm (¼in) wide ribbon. Gather about 10cm (4in) of narrow lace and draw up to form a rosette. Stitch the rose in the centre. Cut green ribbon in half, place the two pieces together and fold in half. Stitch fold to centre front of sash, with the rose on top.

9. Turn up the hem and stitch, then trim with narrow lace, overlapping the edge.

SLEEPING BEAUTY'S HAIR DECORATION AND NECKBAND

10. Cut each length of pearls in half and place the four strings together, twisting at the centre. Wind the twisted centre around the base of the top-knot and make a single knot, allowing the ends to hang freely at each side. Tuck a single flower under the knotted pearls, then fix two or more in the hair at each side of the face,

11. Fix 3mm (⅛in) ribbon around neck as illustrated and join at back.

SLEEPING BEAUTY'S ROSE-TRIMMED SLIPPERS

12. Follow the directions in Basics 10, using the patterns for Alice's shoes. Then trim each with a rose made as step 8.

Prince Florimund

Since fairytales were first invented, children have listened spellbound to the well-loved stories of romance and chivalry. And what little girl hasn't dreamed of waking up to find a handsome prince in her bedroom? Now is her chance to realise that ambition. Here is a handsome storybook hero for little girls of any age who still believe in fairytales.

MATERIALS

Two 30cm (12in) squares of flesh felt
One 30cm (12in) square of dark beige felt
50g (2oz) ball of dark brown double-knit yarn, for hair
For other materials, see Basics 8, items 1–9 inclusive

35cm (⅜yd) deep rose felt, 90cm (36in) wide, for coat and breeches
30 × 25cm (12 × 10in) wine felt, for waistcoat (vest) and coat trimmings

12 × 20cm (4½ × 8in) black felt, for shoes
15 × 65cm (6 × 25in) light-weight white cotton-type fabric, for shirt
1.5m (1½yd) white lace, 30mm (1–1¼in) deep
1m (1yd) very narrow lace to trim coat (optional)
60cm (⅝yd) narrow black braid
1m (1yd) narrow crimson braid
50cm (½yd) single-face black satin ribbon, 9mm (⅜in) wide
5 tiny silver beads, for waistcoat buttons
2 silver sequins, 15mm (⅝in) diameter (optional) and 2 tiny black beads (optional) to trim shoes
'Ruby' diamanté (rhinestone) or similar jewel for cravat
20cm (8in) white bias binding
30cm (12in) narrow round elastic
6 snap-fasteners
Matching threads
Clear adhesive

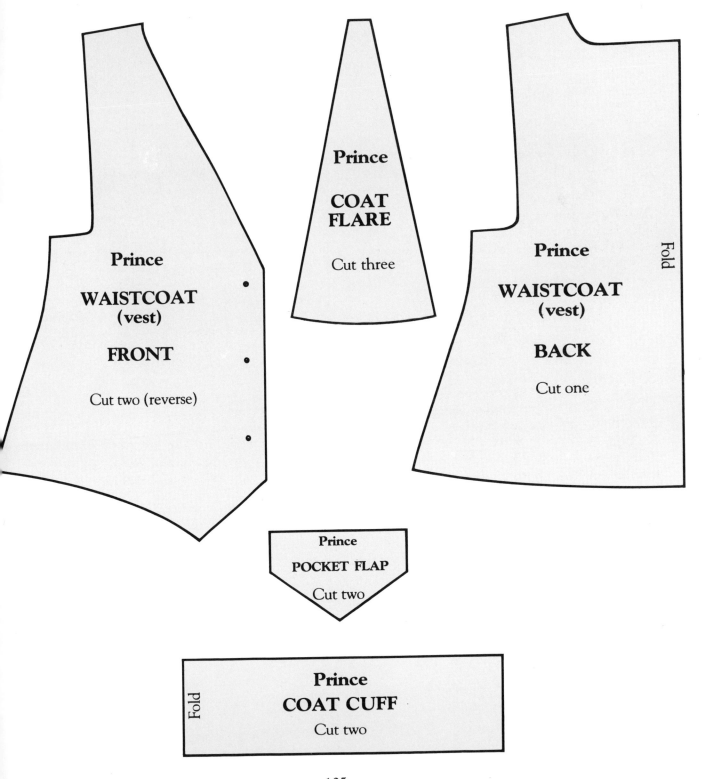

Prince

**WAISTCOAT
(vest)**

FRONT

Cut two (reverse)

Prince

**COAT
FLARE**

Cut three

Prince

**WAISTCOAT
(vest)**

BACK

Cut one

Fold

Prince
POCKET FLAP
Cut two

Fold

Prince
COAT CUFF
Cut two

PRINCE FLORIMUND: THE BASIC FIGURE

Follow the directions for the basic Fairytale Doll on page 19, but cut the legs and soles in beige felt. Use blue sequins for the eyes. For Prince Florimund's hair, see Basics 9.

PRINCE FLORIMUND'S LACE-TRIMMED SHIRT

1. Follow the directions for the Mad Hatter's shirt (page 53), noting the cutting line for the sleeve. Complete steps 1, 2, 3, 4 and 6, omitting step 5.
2. Turn under the raw lower edge of each sleeve, then make a 1cm (⅜in) hem. Stitch the top edge of wide lace close to the edge of the sleeve, so that it hangs down below. Then gather a 23cm (9in) length of lace and stitch over the first layer, drawing up the gathers evenly around the sleeve.
3. Thread the elastic through the hems and draw up to fit the arms.
4. Cut a 35cm (14in) length of white lace for his cravat. Mark the centre and turn under the cut edges, then gather the straight edge. Draw up quite tightly, folding in half and placing the gathers side by side, so that the gathered area measures about 2cm (¾in). Catch together neatly. Stitch to the shirt front, over the snap-fasteners, the ends of the gathers level with the neck binding.

Finally, join the cut ends of a 23cm (9in) length of lace, then gather the straight edge. Draw up very tightly to form a rosette and stitch over top of previous lace. Gather out and back between the centre and top edge of the rosette and draw up tightly, to hold lace neatly down under chin.

Stitch diamanté (rhinestone) or alternative trim in centre of the rosette.

PRINCE FLORIMUND'S ROSE FELT BREECHES

5. Follow the directions in Basics 10.

PRINCE FLORIMUND'S BRAIDED WAISTCOAT (VEST)

6. Cut the back once and the front twice in wine felt. Join the shoulder and side seams. Turn to the right side.
7. Stitch snap-fasteners down the centre front at the points indicated with an O.
8. Glue narrow black braid close to the edge, beginning and ending under the centre front opening.
9. Stitch silver bead 'buttons' down the centre front, as illustrated.

PRINCE FLORIMUND'S COAT

10. Using the pattern for the March Hare's frock coat (page 55), cut the back once, and the front and sleeve twice each in rose felt. Cut the Prince's cuff and pocket flap twice each in wine felt.
11. Cut the Prince's skirt flare three times. Cut the back of the coat along the fold line to make two pieces. Oversew the side edge of one flare to one of the back pieces along the edge you have just cut, keeping the lower edges level. Then oversew the two back pieces together again, taking in the flare. (*Note*: For the best results, sew this garment by hand.)

Stitch another flare to each side edge of the back, keeping the lower edges level.
12. Oversew the front pieces to the back at each shoulder.
13. Fit the sleeves into the armholes of the coat as described for the shirt, but gather close to the edge of the felt, and don't clip the curve. Oversew the sleeve and side seams, taking in the flares. Turn to the right side and press all the seams flat.
14. Turn up the lower edge of each sleeve 5mm (¼in). Glue a cuff to this edge, the lower edge of the cuff overlapping the fold about 2mm (1/16in). Glue the overlap. Glue black braid around the top edge.
15. Glue black braid around the side and lower edges of each pocket flap, then glue to the coat fronts as illustrated (this is a little closer to the side seam than marked on the pattern).
16. Stitch narrow lace around the front and lower edges of the coat as illustrated, keeping the straight edge level with the edge of the felt. Then glue crimson braid around the edge of the coat, over your stitches.

PRINCE FLORIMUND'S BUCKLED SHOES

17. Follow the directions in Basics 10.
18. To trim each shoe, make another bow as before, then stitch a silver sequin in the centre, anchoring it with a tiny black bead. Stitch to the front. (*Note*: The sequins may be omitted, or they may be glued on, omitting the beads.)

CHAPTER 8

A Visitor at Honeysuckle Cottage

When the bears arrived home they were dismayed to find the door unlocked.

'Perhaps there are burglars inside!' whispered Baby Bear.

Father Bear picked up a heavy piece of wood and crept stealthily in, followed by Mother Bear, with Baby Bear holding on to her skirt, his eyes tightly shut.

Three porridge bowls were on the table.

'Who's been eating my porridge?' Father Bear said in surprise.

'And mine?' exclaimed Mother Bear.

'And who's been eating *mine*?' shouted Baby Bear indignantly. 'Because whoever it is has finished it all up!'

'Someone's been sitting in my chair!' Father Bear remarked in a puzzled voice.

Mother Bear turned to look at *her* chair: 'And in mine!' she said.

'And in my chair!' squeaked Baby Bear, bouncing up and down on the cushioned seat to make sure that it wasn't broken.

Father Bear called from the bedroom: 'Someone's been sleeping in our bed!'

Then Baby Bear shouted: 'Someone is still asleep in *my* bed!'

Mr and Mrs Bear rushed over to look, and they both laughed with relief.

'It's Goldilocks!' smiled Father Bear, as Baby Bear's little cousin woke up and rubbed her eyes.

'I'm sorry,' she yawned, 'but I caught an earlier bus. You were out when I arrived and I found the key under the mat. I was so tired and hungry that I had some porridge and fell asleep.'

So the day ended happily, with Baby Bear telling Goldilocks all his adventures in the woods. Goldilocks wanted to go for another picnic, to see if she could find the brown butterfly. But Baby Bear thought it would be too dangerous for her because she wasn't as brave as he was.

Goldilocks suspected she was a great deal braver than Baby Bear, but she was too polite to mention the fact.

Instead, they had a wonderful time playing together every day in the garden of Honeysuckle Cottage where all the butterflies were white and never flew anywhere more interesting than Father Bear's cabbage patch.

Making the Furniture: Materials and Methods

Father Bear's main occupation is bee-keeping, and Mother Bear spends most of her time cooking, so they had no previous experience in making furniture. As there are few things more painful than hitting one's paw with a hammer, the bears decided glue was preferable to nails. The sticky stuff *can* make a nasty mess of your fur, of course – but not if you're careful. Sawing a straight line through a piece of wood can be tricky too, if you're not an expert. So the bears agreed that, used with care, a sharp knife would be a lot easier. And wood can be expensive; so they thought very hard, and managed to avoid that, too. How did they do it?

They took their wheelbarrow down to the local supermarket and collected all the empty grocery delivery cartons they could carry. When the supermarket ran out, they begged a few more from friendly small shopkeepers. While Father Bear cut the stiff corrugated card, Mother cut the fabric; then they both had a paw in gluing it all together. Occasionally, they needed some medium-weight plain card too, but this was no problem because there's never any shortage of cereal cartons in Honeypot Cottage. As well as all that porridge, Baby Bear is very fond of cornflakes, and the packets they come in are ideal for furniture-making.

ESSENTIAL EQUIPMENT

With so little skill, such basic materials and only a few simple tools, the Three Bears produced all the furniture that is illustrated here. The secret is great care and accuracy in measuring and cutting each piece of card, so that everything fits together perfectly at the end. As long as you observe this simple rule, you can be sure of success. The most important pieces of equipment are a straight-edge metal rule (plastic or wood won't do) and a very sharp craft knife (one with snap-off blades is a good idea as you can keep renewing the tip of the knife as it becomes blunt – the Olfa knife is ideal).

Plenty of graph paper, a sharp pencil and a ruler are the other essentials (and some paper-cutting scissors if you want to preserve your sewing ones), plus a good cutting surface. If you feel it is too extravagant to cut the graph paper to make your patterns, you can tape a piece of tracing paper down over the graph paper and draw your patterns on that. But the advantage of using the graph paper itself is that it is stiff enough to draw round and use as a template. You can rule your own squared paper, but there is the danger of distortion if the measurements are not absolutely accurate.

CHOOSING THE CARTONS

Select your corrugated cartons carefully – you will soon learn how to discriminate. Look out for sturdy, good quality boxes. The card should be firm, flat and rigid, not soft or flattened in use. Ones which have held bottles are often particularly good (wines and spirits are nearly always packed in excellent cartons, so try your off-licence too). Reject any carton which is dirty or badly stained, which retains the smell of its contents, which has greasy marks, or which has held soap powder. Damaged cartons are usually not worth consideration, but if they are just the kind of card you are looking for, you may find you can salvage one or two sides. It is usually best to have the ridges in the corrugated card running vertically, but if you can't avoid them going horizontally, it won't matter.

You shouldn't have any difficulty finding suitable cartons from which to cut most of the pieces to make the furniture, but in one or two cases, quite large pieces are needed. Items such as washing-machines and television sets are usually delivered in very large, good-quality boxes. So, if you're not planning to buy any new domestic equipment at the moment, make sure your friends know about your strange collecting habits, just in case *they* are! (The danger here is that you may find yourself overwhelmed with useless cartons generously donated by kind neighbours. If this happens, thank them warmly, then chop up the boxes and wait for a dark night to fill your dustbin with the pieces. *Never* discourage free gifts – you don't know what you might get next time!)

CUTTING LARGE PIECES

If you are unable to find a carton big enough, tape two pieces of card together (make sure that both edges are cut very clean and straight, so that they fit together perfectly). Better still, cut out the pattern shape twice in the thinnest corrugated card you can find. In each case, join two pieces of card, as described above, but make your joins fall in completely different places. Then glue the two shapes together so that you have one double-thickness piece of card, each side reinforcing the join in the other.

SCORING LINES

When you have to score a line (indicated by a broken line on the pattern), do it on both sides of the card. This must be very accurate to be properly aligned, so when you have scored one side with a blunt knife, push a pin straight through the scored card about 5mm (¼in) from each end of the line. Then turn the card over to score the other side, pushing your ruler against the pin-pricks.

DRAWING YOUR PATTERNS

In most cases, because of the size of the furniture, it is not possible to give actual-size patterns, but the shapes are so simple that it is very easy to draw your own patterns following the diagrams. Use graph paper, or else rule squares, but do make sure that they are 100 per cent accurate. The scale of the diagrams is 2cm or 1in to the square (there are separate diagrams for metric and imperial). To make the job even easier, the actual measurements are shown on the diagram wherever they don't line up exactly with the squares.

Although precise measurements are given, these cannot take into account the exact thickness of the actual card you will be using. So to make quite certain that your pieces will fit together well, it is wise to check them against each other as you go along, then you can make any slight adjustments necessary, especially if using imperial measurements.

PREPARATION AND THE RIGHT ADHESIVES

If your fabric has a white ground, it is a good idea to mask the card pieces with white lining paper before covering them with the fabric. This is also a wise precaution if the card is heavily printed, although, as explained later, in most cases two pieces of card are stuck together to form a double-thickness, so you can use the unprinted inside for the outer faces.

A white PVA adhesive is the most economical glue for most jobs. Used quite generously, it will bond both card and fabric together strongly. However, you will probably find it quicker and easier to stick the braid trimming on with clear adhesive. Also, although it is not essential, you may find it helpful, when you are covering a piece of card with fabric, to 'anchor' the fabric to the right side of the card with a dry-stick adhesive (glue stick), which looks like a giant lipstick, lightly rubbed over the surface (see Basics 1).

COVERING THE PIECES

To cover your cut-out shapes with fabric, place the card right side down on the wrong side of your fabric (fixing it with a glue stick, as described above, if you wish), then cut the fabric about 15mm (⅝in) away from the edge of the card. Study figures 1 and 2 for Mother Bear's armchair (see page 117) for examples of the various techniques for preparing the surplus fabric around the edge of the card. First cut off the corners diagonally, just a fraction away from the edge of the card. Then snip any inward curves and cut V-shaped notches in outward curves. Always cut almost to the edge of the card – but not quite (about 3mm (⅛in), but be guided by the thickness of your fabric).

Run a trail of adhesive about 1cm (⅜in) from one edge of the card. Lift the surplus fabric up, taking it smoothly around the card, and press it down into the adhesive. Glue each piece of overlapping fabric to the back of the card in the same way, drawing it smoothly round so that it is absolutely flat and even on the right side. Leave any tabs until last, but stick in exactly the same way.

PADDED UPHOLSTERY

If the piece you are covering needs to be padded, use medium-weight (4oz) polyester wadding. To make seats and mattresses more deeply cushioned, you can use heavier wadding, but a double thickness of medium-weight is just as good. Glue the right side of the card to your wadding and leave it to dry. Then trim the wadding just a fraction away from the edge of the card all round – about 3–5mm (⅛–¼in).

Cover the padded pieces in the same way, but allow a little more surplus fabric to overlap all round the edge: 2.5cm (1in) is usually about right, but it will depend somewhat on the thickness of your fabric.

CONSTRUCTION AND ASSEMBLY

In most instances, you will be gluing two covered pieces together to form each section of the piece of furniture you are making. Use your glue quite liberally on the back of one piece (the smaller, if the two pieces are different sizes), spreading it over to make sure that it doesn't drip, and then run a trail quite close to the edge. Press the two pieces very firmly together and hold them until they are firmly stuck (concentrate on the edges: the centre doesn't matter much, as long as you have spread it with glue).

Then all you have to do is to assemble the piece of furniture as explained in the directions and cover any unsightly joins with braid. Should you have difficulty in finding the colour you want to complement your fabric, you could make your own from ribbon (see Basics 6). If one plait is not wide enough, glue two side by side.

CHOOSING THE RIGHT FABRIC

As a guide to choosing your own covering fabric, you will see that the type of fabric illustrated is always clearly described, but generally, a light-weight furnishing fabric, or a medium-weight dress fabric, will be most suitable. Don't choose sheer, or very thin, fabrics, or ones which are thick and bulky or loosely woven. Avoid totally synthetic fabrics, as they may be difficult to stick. A certain amount of natural fibre (ideally cotton) is desirable. The pretty 'Wild Clematis' design which Mother Bear chose to echo her wallpaper is Laura Ashley's Country Furnishing Cotton, which is lovely to work with, as well as to look at.

If you want to experiment with something very easy for your first venture, try Baby Bear's cradle bed. The directions for that are especially detailed so that you won't even need to refer back to this section if you don't remember any of the techniques described above.

HOW TO MAKE YOUR OWN CYLINDRICAL BASES

It is sometimes expedient to use a firm cylinder as the basis for a piece of furniture. The bears' table, for example, stands on an empty cardboard canister which formerly contained a well-known brand of table salt. The Saxa table salt pack happens to be particularly suitable for this purpose, but there are usually plenty of containers around the house which could be utilised when they are empty. Plastic washing-up liquid or lemonade bottles can be cut down, although they are very light and need to be weighted.

However, it is often quicker and easier to make your own cylinder, as you can then choose exactly the height and diameter you want. And, even more important, you can also give it much more weight than a plastic container, so that it stands firm and steady. All you need is plenty of clean, flat waste paper. Good quality magazines and catalogues are excellent, old sheets of cartridge-weight drawing paper are even better, and a leftover roll of wallpaper is wonderful. The larger the cylinder, the stiffer your paper should be: for a diameter of 10cm (4in) or more, you can use cereal cartons.

1. First find a piece of fairly thin card (cereal or crispbread packet) which is at least 2.5cm (1in) larger all round than the diameter of the cylinder you are planning to make. Cut a circle in the centre of the card, exactly the diameter of the cylinder you require.
2. Cut numerous strips of smooth, flat paper (of the type described above). Each strip should be the depth of your cylinder and at least 30cm (12in) long (for a diameter of more than 8cm (3in) it will need to be even longer).
3. Roll up one strip of paper, place it inside the circle and allow it to open out so that it fits snugly against the cut edge of the hole. Remove and glue the overlap.
4. Roll up another strip of paper and repeat inside the cylinder made by the first strip, edge to edge with the previous strip. Make sure that the top and bottom edges are exactly level. Lightly glue the new strip to the last one to hold it in place.
5. Continue, adding several sheets at a time, until you have built up a firm, strong shell. It doesn't matter how much paper you roll up inside – it all helps to make your base solid and steady.

Baby Bear's Cradle-Bed

When Baby Bear needed a bed, Mother and Father Bear put their heads together and came up with this very simple design. Being sensible parents, they planned ahead to allow for growth – which is why Goldilocks found it just the right size for her, too. Bears apart, this would make a lovely doll's cradle – all for the cost of the fabric and glue, plus as little or as much trimming as you want to add.

The fabric used is a firm cotton sheeting: this is ideal for the purpose and very easy to work with. However, any medium-weight cotton-type fabric would do; a firm dress fabric or a light-weight furnishing fabric would be equally suitable. If you choose one of these, increase the length shown below in the list of materials, according to the width of the fabric.

A white PVA adhesive is best for gluing the fabric to the card. You can use PVA adhesive to stick on the braid too, but a tube of all-purpose clear adhesive makes the job even easier.

MATERIALS

Corrugated cardboard
60cm (¾yd) cotton sheeting, 228cm (90in) wide, for the bed and coverlet
40cm (½yd) medium-weight cotton-type fabric, 90cm (36in) wide, for the sheet and pillow
2.8m (3¼yd) narrow braid, about 8–10mm (¼–⅜in) wide, to match your covering fabric
1.25m (1⅜yd) lace, 10mm (⅜in) wide, to trim the sheet and pillow
1.5m (1¾yd) double-face satin ribbon, 9mm (⅜in) wide, to trim the bed and coverlet
20cm (¼yd) single-face satin ribbon, 6mm (¼in) wide, to trim the pillow
70cm (⅞yd) medium-weight (4oz) polyester wadding, 90cm (36in) wide
Polyester stuffing
Matching threads
Adhesive tape
PVA adhesive
Clear adhesive

Note: If you are using sheeting for the bed, as suggested, choose a design which can be used sideways, then turn your length of fabric to give you a selvedge along the top edge so that, when you cut your first side piece (step 3), the top edge of your piece of fabric will be the selvedge. Continue to work down the strip of fabric in this way, cutting the end pieces side by side, until you reach the bottom (the other selvedge), where you will have enough left to make the coverlet.

1. Begin by making an 'upside-down box' for the base. Following the measurements shown in figure 1, cut two pieces of card for the sides, two pieces for the ends and one large piece for the top. Tape the sides between the ends, then rest the top over them and tape it securely in place. (If your card is rather thin and you want to make a firmer base, just add one or two more layers of card taped on top.) Now cut four corner reinforcing pieces as shown in figure 2. Score down the centre, as indicated by the broken line, then bend around to form a right angle and glue one inside each corner of the box. (Again, add more strips inside to strengthen the sides and ends of the box if your card is thin.) Set this aside while you prepare the sides and ends of the bed.

2. Make patterns for the head and the foot, then cut two pieces of card for each. Cut four pieces for the sides, to the measurements shown in figure 3.

3. For the inside of the bed, cut pieces of fabric to cover two of the side pieces to the measurements shown in figure 4. Place the fabric right side down on a flat surface, with the card, plain side down, on top (as indicated in the diagram). Snip off the corners of the fabric diagonally, as indicated by the broken lines, just a fraction away from the corners of the card.

Run a trail of adhesive along the top of the card, about 1cm (⅜in) from the edge. Lift the surplus fabric up, taking it smoothly over the edge of the card, and press it down into the adhesive. Glue the lower edge of the fabric to the back of the card in the same way, drawing it smoothly round so that it is absolutely flat and even on the right side. Finally, glue the side edges round in exactly the same way.

4. For the outside of the bed, cut pieces of fabric to cover the other two side pieces as shown in figure 5. Place the card on the wrong side of the fabric as before, with an equal surplus (2.5cm/1in) at the top and sides. Snip off the top corners and then glue the fabric at the top and sides to the card as

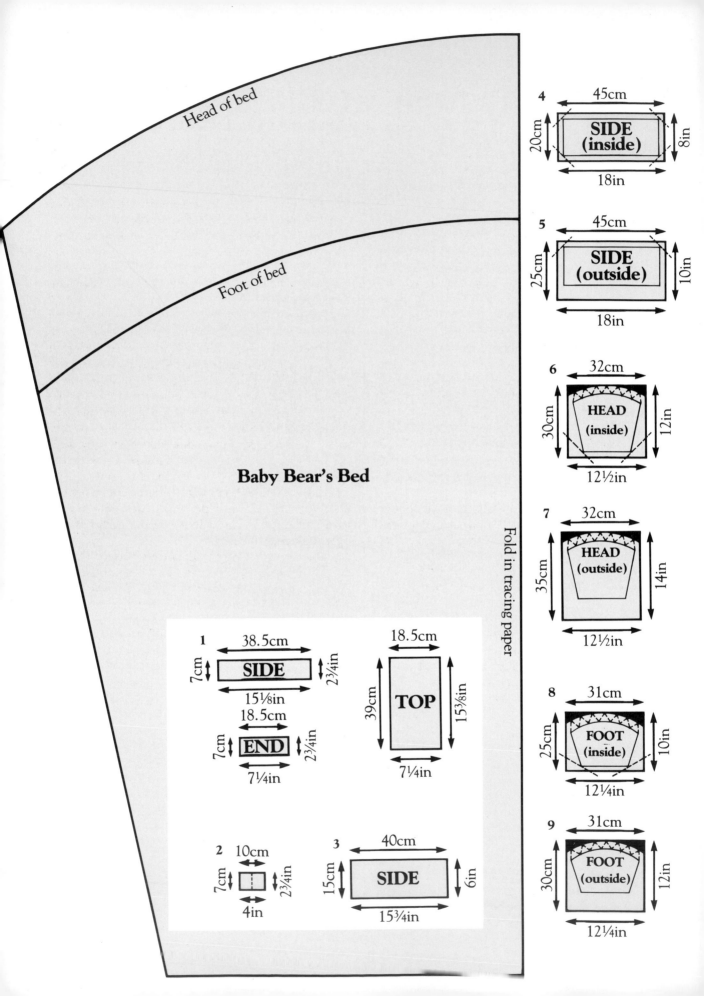

Head of bed

Foot of bed

Baby Bear's Bed

Fold in tracing paper

4 45cm
20cm **SIDE (inside)** 8in
18in

5 45cm
25cm **SIDE (outside)** 10in
18in

6 32cm
30cm **HEAD (inside)** 12in
12½in

7 32cm
35cm **HEAD (outside)** 14in
12½in

8 31cm
25cm **FOOT (inside)** 10in
12¼in

9 31cm
30cm **FOOT (outside)** 12in
12¼in

1 38.5cm
7cm **SIDE** 2¾in
15⅛in

18.5cm
7cm **END** 2¾in
7¼in

18.5cm
39cm **TOP** 15⅜in
7¼in

2 10cm
7cm 2¾in
4in

3 40cm
15cm **SIDE** 6in
15¾in

described in step 3, but leave free the excess fabric at the bottom.

6. Glue an inside piece very securely to an outside piece, making sure that the edges of the card are absolutely level, with the surplus fabric on the outside piece flapping below. Leave on an even surface weighted down with some large books so that it dries perfectly flat.

7. Cut a piece of fabric for the inside of the bed-head as shown in figure 6. Snip away the two bottom corners as indicated by the broken lines, then glue the excess fabric along the lower edge to the card in the usual way, followed by the two sides. Now cut away the fabric at the top corners in a curve (see the shaded areas on the diagram). Trim off the excess overlap at the top of each side, then snip out V-shaped notches as indicated. Glue the resulting tabs to the back of the card, taking the fabric smoothly over the edge as before.

8. Cut a piece of fabric for the outside of the bed-head as shown in figure 7. Don't trim off any corners, but position the card on the fabric as indicated, then glue the sides, followed by the top, exactly as described in step 7. Leave free the surplus at the bottom as before. Allow to dry under a weight, as for the sides of the bed.

9. Cut the fabric to cover the inside of the foot of the bed as shown in figure 8. Follow the directions for the bed-head as described in step 7.

10. Cut the fabric to cover the outside of the foot of the bed as shown in figure 9. Follow the directions for the bed-head (as described in step 8).

11. Glue the braid neatly all round the side and top edges of all four pieces over the join.

12. Return to the base of the bed and cut two or three layers of wadding 39 × 30cm (15½ × 12in). Glue these to the top of the base, keeping the edges level with the two ends, but overlapping equally at each side. Roll these side pieces tightly round into a sausage at each side (keeping them level with the top) and catch with a few stitches to hold their shape. Cut a piece of fabric to measure 50 × 36cm (20 × 14in). Place it right side up over the wadding. Glue the overlapping edges smoothly down, first over the ends, then over the sides of the base, folding the corners in neatly and finally catching the fabric together at each corner with a few stitches when the glue is dry.

13. Now you are ready to assemble the bed. Begin with the head: spread the glue liberally over one end of the base, then press the inside of the head against it, keeping the lower edges of the head and base absolutely level and the corners matching. When the head is firmly glued in position, fold in the corners of the surplus fabric at the bottom so that you can glue it neatly up inside the base. Use plenty of glue to do this.

14. Glue the foot of the bed into position in exactly the same way.

15. For each side, run a generous trail of glue close to the lower edge of the side of the base, then press the inside of the side piece against it, the lower edges and corners matching as for the head. Holding the side securely in this position, glue the surplus fabric at the bottom inside the base as before.

16. Stitch the top corner of each side very securely to the edge of the head or foot, at the point where they meet, then cut a 30cm (12in) length of ribbon for each corner and stitch the centre over your previous stitches. Tie the ribbons into four bows.

17. To make the coverlet, cut two 30cm (12in) squares of fabric and a 28cm (11in) square of wadding. Tack the wadding to the wrong side of one piece of fabric, leaving an equal overlap all round. Pin the two pieces of fabric right sides together, then join all round, stitching level with the edge of the wadding and leaving a 10cm (4in) opening at the centre of one side. Clip the corners and turn to the right side. Slip stitch the edges of the opening neatly together.

18. Make a line of stitching all round the coverlet, about 3cm (1¼in) from the outer edge, to form a quilted border. Then make two butterfly bows from 12.5cm (5in) of the matching ribbon (see Basics 6: mark points B 3.5cm (1⅜in) from A), and stitch one at each lower corner of the stitching line which you have just completed.

19. Cut a piece of fabric to measure 50 × 45cm (20 × 16in) for the sheet, if possible using the selvedge for the short (top) edge. Turn under all the raw edges and make a narrow hem. Trim the top edge with lace.

20. Cut two pieces of fabric to measure 15 × 24cm (6 × 9½in) for the pillow. Keeping the right sides together, join them all round, leaving 5cm (2in) open at the centre of one short side. Clip the corners and turn to the right side. Stuff to the thickness required, then slip stitch the opening.

21. Stitch lace all round the edge of the pillow, gathering neatly at each corner. Then make two bows (using the same method as the ones for the coverlet) from 10cm (4in) narrow ribbon (see Basics 6: mark points B 3cm (1¼in) from A). Stitch one at each top corner of the pillow.

The Bears' Victorian Table

Mother Bear gets very nostalgic when she uses this small round table with its dainty gathered skirt, because it reminds her of one her great-grandmother owned, though great-grandma's table was not made from cardboard boxes and Laura Ashley Furnishing Cotton.

The base is a cardboard canister which originally contained table salt; but if you're on a salt-free diet, don't worry. Either find a similar container or roll up lots of waste paper, as explained on page 112.

MATERIALS

Corrugated cardboard
Medium-weight card (cereal carton)
Cylindrical container, about 15cm (6in) high, or alternative (see above)
25cm (10in) fabric, 115cm (45in) wide to cover or 45cm (18in) fabric, 90cm (36in) wide
65cm (¾yd) narrow matching braid (about 8–10cm (¼–⅜in) wide), to trim
Matching thread
Paper to cover cylinder (optional)
PVA adhesive
Clear adhesive

1. Cut four 18cm (7in) diameter circles of corrugated card and one of plain card. Glue three of the corrugated circles together. Glue the plain one on top of the remaining corrugated one.
2. Cut a 23cm (9in) diameter circle of fabric. Place the fabric right side down, with the second of the above circles on top, keeping the plain card side down. Make sure that the fabric overlaps equally all round (if you have some dry-stick adhesive, use this to hold the card circle in place). About 5cm (2in) at a time, spread PVA adhesive generously quite close to the edge of the card, then bring the fabric smoothly up and over the edge of the card, and press it down into the adhesive, gathering it neatly with your fingertips as you do so. Continue to pat it down into place until it is firmly held.
3. Cut a piece of fabric for the skirt, 20cm (8in deep) × 90cm (36in) wide. Join the short side edges and press the seam open. Turn to the right side. Mark the top equally into eight, then gather 1cm (⅜in) below the edge.
4. Rule four straight lines across the top of the first card circle, dividing it into eight equal sections (like a cake). Pin the top edge of the fabric round the cut edge of the card circle, matching the marked points to the ends of the lines and drawing up the gathers to fit. As in step 2, spread the adhesive close to the edge of the card and then glue the top edge of the gathered fabric neatly down.
5. Place the skirt section on top of your base and turn up the hem to the correct length. Remove and stitch neatly, then replace, this time gluing it very firmly into place.
6. Glue the covered circle on top of the skirt section. Use clear adhesive to glue the braid over the skirt gathers, close under the top.

Mother Bear's Comfortable Armchair

Mrs Bear likes her armchair for its elegant lines, its softly padded interior and the fact that it is just the right shape for her comfortable figure. With her keen eye for tasteful decor, she upholstered her chair with the same reverse print of the wallpaper that she chose for the curtains and the tablecloth.

Very careful measuring and cutting will ensure that all your pieces fit together perfectly, and if you have mastered the simple technique of padding and covering the pieces of card, you can't go wrong.

MATERIALS

Corrugated cardboard
Medium-weight card (cereal carton)
50cm (½yd) light-weight furnishing fabric or medium-weight dress fabric, 115cm (45in) wide *or* 60cm (24in) fabric, 90cm (36in) wide
2m (2yd) narrow braid, about 8–10mm (¼–⅜in) wide, to match your fabric
35 × 70cm (14 × 24in) medium-weight (4oz) polyester wadding
Matching thread
Adhesive tape
PVA adhesive
Clear adhesive

Using graph paper (or ruling squares), draw out your patterns following the diagram for Mother Bear's armchair. Diagram A is for metric measurements (each square equals 2cm); diagram B is for imperial measurements (each square equals 1in).

1. In corrugated card, cut the outer back, the inner back and the seat once each, and the outer arm and the inner arm twice each (reverse the outer and inner arm patterns to cut the second piece in each case). Score the outer back and the outer arms as indicated by the broken lines.

Cut the under-seat and the front once each in medium-weight card. For Mother Bear and Father Bear, fit the front around the curved front edge of the under-seat to check that the length is exactly the same; if it is not, correct.

2. Pad the inner back and the two inner arms with one layer of wadding (remembering that the second arm is reversed). Pad the seat with two layers of wadding. Cover all three pieces with fabric, as described on page 111, snipping the surplus as shown in figure 1 (for the inner arm of Father Bear's chair, see figure 1a, page 123).

3. Cover the outer back with fabric (snip the surplus as shown in figure 2). Cover each outer arm also (remembering that the second piece is reversed), but turn the fabric over the top, bottom and front edges only. Leave the surplus at the back free (for Father Bear, snip the upper section as shown in figure 1a). Cover the front too, but don't turn over the top edge.

4. Glue an inner arm to each outer arm, matching the top and side edges very carefully.

5. Keeping right sides together and with corners matching, oversew the bottom edge of the inner back piece to the back edge of the seat.

6. Make the base as follows. Cut one piece of corrugated card each for the front and the back, and two pieces for the sides, as shown in figure 3 (for Father Bear, follow figure 5 page 122; for Baby Bear, see figure 6 page 123). Tape the four pieces temporarily together at each corner, fixing the side pieces between the front and the back. Cut four corner pieces as shown in figure 4 (for Baby Bear, as shown in figure 7, page 123). Score each one as indicated by the broken line and bend at right angles. Glue one inside each corner of the base. Remove the tape (it may prevent the fabric from sticking later). Cut several more strips of corrugated card to fit inside the front of the base and glue them into position (this will add weight and correct the balance of the chair).

7. Glue the under-seat to the top of the base. For Mother and Father Bear, cut V-shaped notches along the overlapping fabric at the top of the front piece (as shown in figure 2). Glue the resulting tabs around the curved front edge of the under-seat.

For Baby Bear, glue the overlapping fabric at the top of the front piece to the front edge of the under-seat.

8. Glue the padded seat on top of the under-seat, then glue the arms to each side of the base. Glue the surplus fabric at the back edge of each arm to the back of the padded inner back piece. Oversew the side edges of the front piece to the front edges of the outer arm pieces.

9. Glue the outer back piece to the inner back and the base. Then oversew each side of the outer back to the back edge of the outer arm.

10. Glue braid over the join between the seat and the front; over the stitched joins between the front and the sides, continuing up over the tops of the arms (for Father Bear, continue up over wing to top of chair); and over the stitched joins between the back and the sides, continuing up over the top of the back.

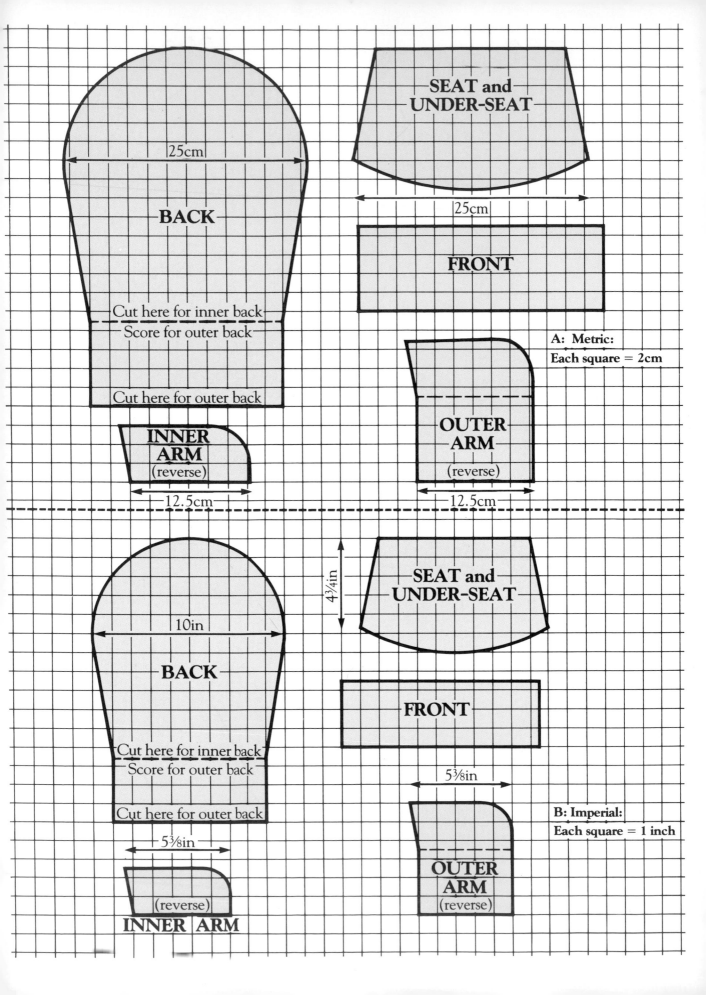

BACK

25cm

Cut here for inner back

Score for outer back

Cut here for outer back

INNER ARM (reverse)

12.5cm

SEAT and UNDER-SEAT

25cm

FRONT

OUTER ARM (reverse)

12.5cm

A: Metric:
Each square = 2cm

BACK

10in

Cut here for inner back

Score for outer back

Cut here for outer back

5⅜in

(reverse)

INNER ARM

4¾in

SEAT and UNDER-SEAT

FRONT

5⅜in

OUTER ARM (reverse)

B: Imperial:
Each square = 1 inch

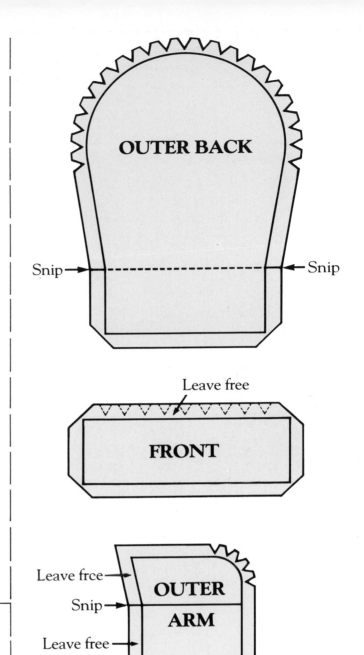

INNER BACK

SEAT

INNER ARM

1

OUTER BACK

Snip → ← Snip

Leave free

FRONT

Leave frce →

Snip →

Leave free →

OUTER ARM

2

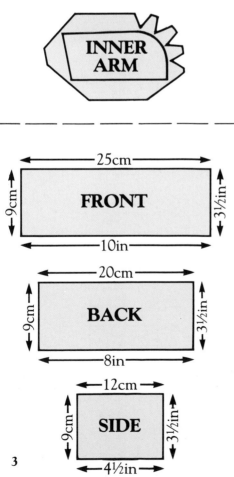

25cm

9cm **FRONT** 3½in

10in

20cm

9cm **BACK** 3½in

8in

12cm

9cm **SIDE** 3½in

4½in

3

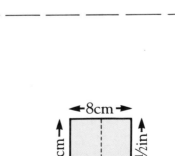

8cm

9cm 3½in

3in

4

Mother Bear's Cushioned Footstool

It's nice to be able to put your feet up after a long day, so when she settles down to knit, Mrs Bear appreciates the small footstool, with its softly cushioned top, which matches her chair. The size, shape and height are all adjustable, so you could make the stool lower or wider if you choose. If you would prefer an oval stool, simply make two cylinders and tape them securely together; then complete the stool as directed for the circular shape, but cut ovals of card to fit the top and bottom of your basic construction and cover them with fabric accordingly.

MATERIALS

Corrugated cardboard
Medium-weight card (cereal carton)
30 × 35cm (12 × 14in) light-weight furnishing fabric or medium-weight dress fabric
70cm (¾yd) narrow braid, about 8–10cm (¼–⅜in) wide, to match your fabric
35cm (⅜yd) silky lampshade fringe, 2.5cm (1in) deep, to match or tone with your fabric and trimming
18 × 24cm (7 × 9½in) medium-weight (4oz) polyester wadding
Matching thread
Adhesive tape
PVA adhesive
Clear adhesive

1. Cut a 10cm (4in) diameter hole in the centre of a piece of card. Cut several strips of flexible card 6cm (2⅜in) wide by at least 34cm (13½in) long and use them to make a cylinder (see page 112). Cut more strips of card (or stiff paper) and fit them inside, to build up a solid foundation and add weight.

2. Cut another length of card, 6cm (2⅜in) deep by the exact circumference of your circle (about 31cm (12in), but measure exactly). Place it on the wrong side of your fabric and cut the fabric so that it overlaps 1.5cm (⅝in) along both long edges and 2cm (¾in) at one short end; cut the other short end level with the card. Bring the surplus fabric smoothly up over the long edges and glue it down onto the card; leave the fabric at the end free. Glue the covered card around your cylinder and glue the overlapping fabric to join.

3. Cut two 10cm (4in) diameter circles of corrugated card for the top and bottom. For the top, glue one circle to a double layer of wadding. When it is dry, cut the wadding just outside the edge of the card. Lift the top layer of wadding and slip another circle, 8cm (3in) in diameter, in the centre between the two layers.

4. Cut an 18cm (7in) diameter circle of fabric and gather all round, quite close to the edge. Place the fabric right side down, with the padded circle, wadding down, in the centre. Draw up the gathers tightly and secure underneath the card. Glue to the top of the cylinder.

5. Cut a 15cm (6in) diameter circle of fabric and, omitting the wadding, cover the other circle of card in exactly the same way, then glue it to the bottom.

6. Glue the fringe and braid around the stool as illustrated, over the joins.

Father Bear's Big Winged Armchair

As head of the household, Father Bear wanted an important-looking chair which gave him a paternal air. This big old-fashioned winged armchair is just the answer when he needs to relax and smoke his pipe after a long and tiring day trying to keep Baby Bear out of mischief. Although it looks so different, the directions are basically the same as for Mother Bear's chair; only the dimensions and the shape are altered.

If you prefer, you could cover it with a fab-

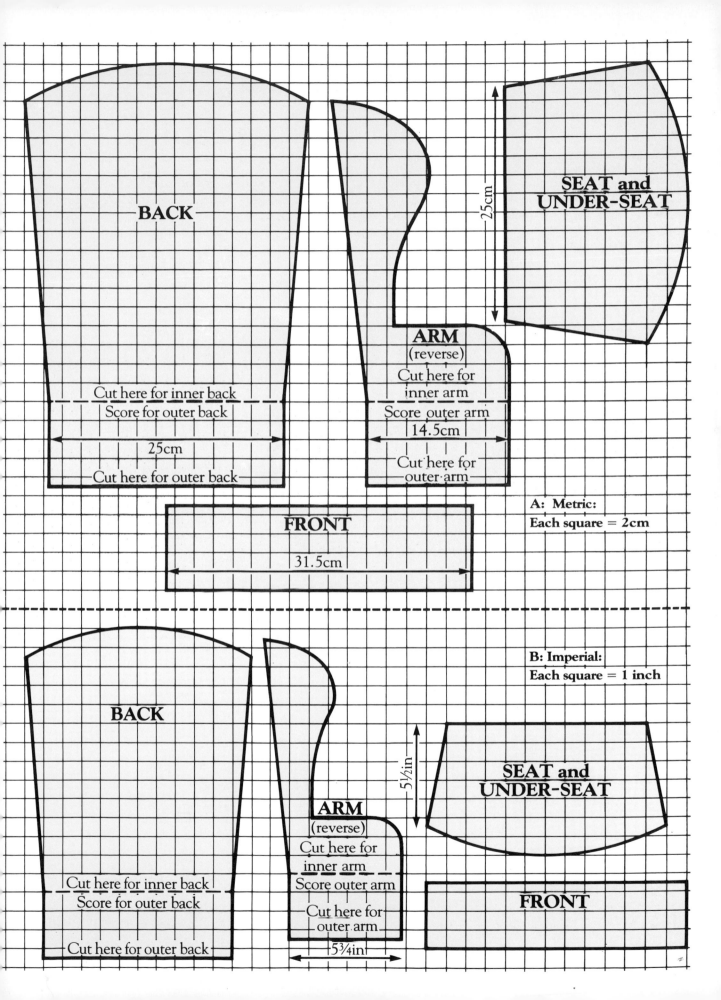

BACK

Cut here for inner back
Score for outer back
25cm
Cut here for outer back

ARM
(reverse)
Cut here for
inner arm
Score outer arm
14.5cm
Cut here for
outer arm

25cm

SEAT and
UNDER-SEAT

FRONT
31.5cm

A: Metric:
Each square = 2cm

B: Imperial:
Each square = 1 inch

BACK

Cut here for inner back
Score for outer back
Cut here for outer back

ARM
(reverse)
Cut here for
inner arm
Score outer arm
Cut here for
outer arm
5¾in

5½in

SEAT and
UNDER-SEAT

FRONT

ric similar to the one Mother Bear chose, but the armchair illustrated is upholstered in a very fine needlecord, which is most effective. You can obtain fine needlecord in either dress- or furnishing-fabric departments, so check the width before you buy.

As you will see below, once you have drawn your patterns, you follow the directions for Mother Bear's chair, with a few slight differences, all of which are clearly indicated. The shape of the pieces in the covering diagrams (figures 1 and 2) will differ slightly, but the principle is the same: just snip and trim the curves and corners as appropriate.

However, you may find it easier to cover the outer arm of this chair completely (step 3), and not leave the fabric along the back edge free to glue to the back of the chair (step 8). If you decide to do this, glue all the edges to the back of the card, as you did for the inner arm. Then, when you glue the pieces to the base (step 8), oversew the back edge of the inner arm to the side edge of the inner back.

MATERIALS

Corrugated cardboard
Medium-weight card (cereal carton)
85cm (1yd) fine needlecord, 115cm (45in) wide *or* 120cm (1⅜yd) fabric, 90cm (36in) wide
2.8m (3⅛yd) furnishing braid, about 10mm (⅜in) wide, to match, or tone with, your fabric
40cm (½yd) medium-weight (4oz) polyester wadding, 90cm (36in) wide
Matching thread
Adhesive tape
PVA adhesive
Clear adhesive

Using graph paper (or ruling squares), draw out your patterns following the diagram for Father Bear's armchair (see pages 121/2). Diagram A is for metric measurements (each square equals 2cm); diagram B is for imperial measurements (each square equals 1in).

Follow the directions for Mother Bear's armchair, steps 1–10.

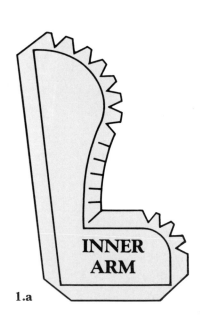

1.a

INNER ARM

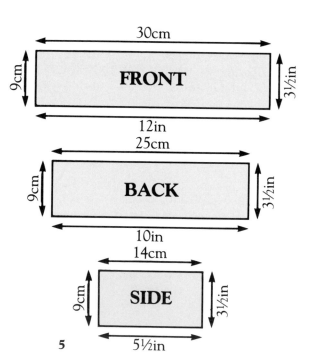

FRONT
30cm
9cm
3½in
12in

BACK
25cm
9cm
3½in
10in

SIDE
14cm
9cm
3½in
5½in

5

Baby Bear's Little Chair

Baby Bear feels very grown-up in the little chair which matches his bed. It's just the right height so that even if he wriggles, he won't have very far to fall and can't hurt himself. Nevertheless, Mother Bear has threatened to fix a ribbon to each arm and to tie him in – so you could do the same, if you think it would be safer.

Once again, after you have drawn your patterns, the method is exactly the same as for Mother Bear's armchair. You can therefore follow the same directions, simply taking in the minor differences and adapting the covering guides (figures 1 and 2) to suit the slightly altered shapes.

The chair illustrated uses the same sheeting as the cradle, but a light-weight furnishing fabric or medium-weight dress fabric would be just as suitable.

MATERIALS

Corrugated cardboard
Medium-weight card (cereal carton)
30cm (12in) light-weight furnishing fabric or medium-weight dress fabric, 115cm (45in) wide *or* 40cm (16in) fabric, 90cm (36in) wide
1.5m (1⅝yd) narrow braid, about 8–10mm (¼–⅜in) wide, to match your fabric
20 × 60cm (8 × 24in) medium-weight (4oz) wadding
Matching thread
Adhesive tape
PVA adhesive
Clear adhesive

Using graph paper (or ruling squares), draw out your patterns following the diagram for Baby Bear's little chair. Diagram A is for metric measurements (each square equals 2cm); diagram B is for imperial measurements (each square equals 1in).

Follow the directions for Mother Bear's armchair, steps 1–10.

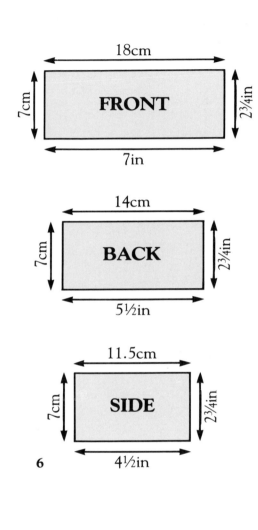

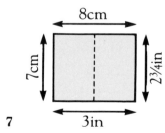

123

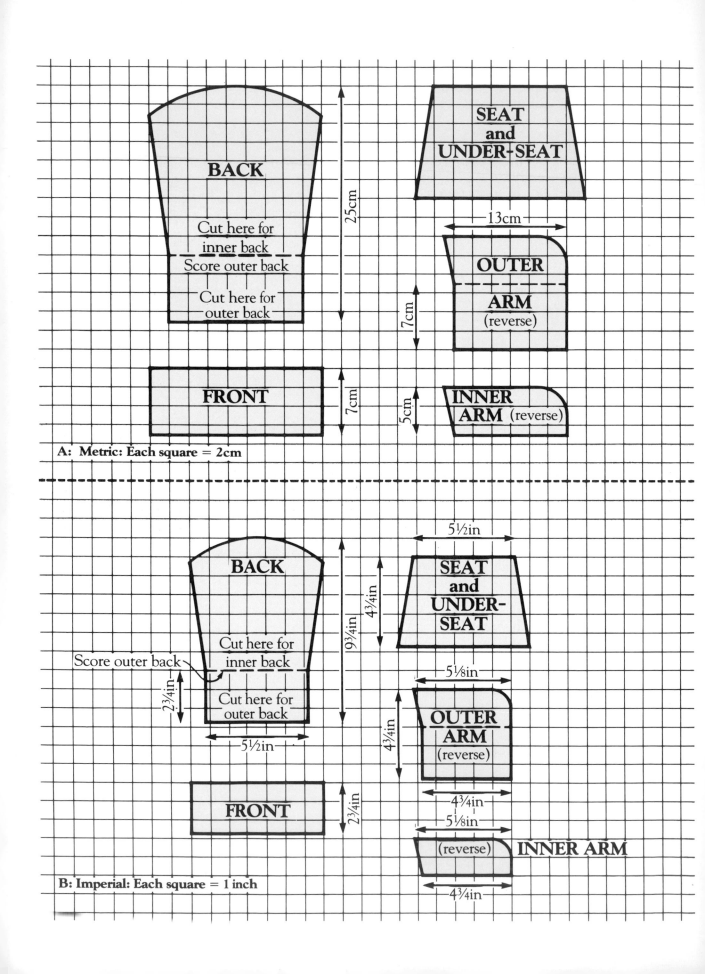

BACK

Cut here for
inner back

Score outer back

Cut here for
outer back

25cm

SEAT
and
UNDER-SEAT

13cm

OUTER
ARM
(reverse)

7cm

FRONT

7cm

5cm

INNER
ARM (reverse)

A: Metric: Each square = 2cm

BACK

Cut here for
inner back

Score outer back

Cut here for
outer back

2¾in

5½in

9¾in

4¾in

SEAT
and
UNDER-
SEAT

5½in

5⅛in

OUTER
ARM
(reverse)

4¾in

FRONT

2¾in

4¾in

5⅛in

(reverse)   INNER ARM

4¾in

B: Imperial: Each square = 1 inch

The Sleeping Beauty's Royal Bed

A romantic bed like this would make any favourite doll's dreams come true. Even if your doll is not a princess, she'll feel like one when she falls asleep under a pink satin sheet beneath a drift of filmy lace-edged curtain which is suspended from a jewelled coronet high above her head.

Find the thickest corrugated board you can, as the bed is bigger than the other furniture and needs to be quite strong. Items such as washing-machines, television sets and self-assembly furniture are often packed in cartons made from double corrugated card and this is ideal.

For the valance and coverlet, choose firmly woven fabrics which won't fray, and try to cut them along the thread, to avoid having to turn up hems. The valance illustrated is made from deep pink cotton sheeting, which does the job beautifully, but any medium-weight cotton-type dress fabric would be just as good. The coverlet is a light-weight lawn-type dress fabric which has a tiny white design printed on a paler pink ground. The theatrical effect is enhanced by the use of several shades of the same colour, frosted with snowy white drapery and lace.

Look for a fairly substantial lace to edge the coverlet. If the lace is too delicate, you may have difficulty stitching it to the gathered fabric. The wide lace for the curtains and bed-linen, however, should be the most delicate and pretty you can find. The lace edge to the valance is an optional extra. It finishes the edge neatly and avoids the necessity of turning up a hem, which might make the frill protrude rather stiffly.

MATERIALS

Corrugated cardboard
Medium-weight white covering paper
10 × 35cm (4 × 14in) thin white card for coronet
Table-salt canister or similar cylindrical container about 15cm (6in) high × 8cm (3in) in diameter
Strip of balsa or thin wood, 63cm (25in) long × 2.5cm (1in) wide
80cm (1yd) deep-pink cotton-type fabric, 90cm (36in) wide, for valance (or 60cm (¾yd) sheeting)
90cm (1yd) pink and white light-weight cotton-type fabric, 90 or 115cm (36 or 45in) wide, for coverlet
90cm (1yd) mid-pink satin, at least 130cm (52in) wide, for bed-head, sheet and pillows

70cm (⅞yd) sheer voile curtain net, 90 or 115cm (36 or 45in) wide
3m (3⅜yd)* pink and white lace, 10mm (⅜in) deep, for coverlet (see above) (*3.5m (4yd) if using wider fabric)
2.3m (2⅝yd) white lace, 20mm (¾in) deep, for valance (optional)
1.6m (1¾yd) white lace, 20mm (¾in) deep, for pillows
5m (5⅝yd) white lace, preferably 30mm (1–1¼in) deep, for curtains, sheet and pillow
75cm (⅞yd) deep-pink, single-face satin ribbon, 9mm (⅜in) wide
85cm (1yd) tiny pearl bead trimming
40cm (½yd) silver/pearl braid, about 10–15mm (½in) wide
70 × 90cm (30 × 36in) medium-weight (4oz) polyester wadding
Polyester stuffing (or use wadding)
Matching threads
Household pins, 25mm (1in) long
Adhesive tape
Wallpaper (or similar) paste (optional)
Dry-stick adhesive
PVA adhesive
Clear adhesive

1. Cut the top of the base, two sides and two ends from corrugated board (see the pattern diagram). Score the broken lines and bend tabs (a) and (b) down. Glue tabs (a) behind the sides, and tabs (b) behind the ends. Cut four small corner pieces of board as shown on the pattern diagram. Score the broken lines and bend at right angles. Fit one inside each corner, below the tabs, to join the sides and ends. Trim the lower edge level before gluing in place. Cut a strip of board to fit inside each side and end, between the corner pieces and below the tabs. Glue in place.
2. Measure the exact size of the top of the base (allowing for the thickness of the sides and ends) and cut a piece of board this size (make a note of these measurements for later use). Glue on top of the base.
3. Paste (or glue) white paper smoothly over the top of the base, overlapping the sides and ends about 4cm (1½in), then cover the sides and ends in the same way.
4. Cut two layers of wadding the same size as the

base. Tack together, then glue lightly on top.

5. For the valance, see the cutting diagram (if using 90cm (36in) wide fabric). First cut a piece of fabric the size of the base plus 1cm (⅜in) extra all round. Then cut four 18cm (7in) deep strips (add 2cm (¾in) if making a hem) across the rest of the fabric for the sides (if using sheeting, cut the side strip first, across the full width of the fabric, then cut the base piece).

6. Make a line of tacking all round the base piece, 1cm (⅜in) from the edge, to indicate the edge of the bed. Add together the measurements of two sides and one end, then divide the result equally into sixteen, marking with pins across the tacking line.

Join the short edges of the side pieces to form one long strip. Mark the top edge equally into sixteen, then gather. Keeping the right sides together, pin the top edge of the strip evenly around the base piece, matching the marked points. Draw up the gathers level with the tacking line and stitch. Trim the corners and turn to the right side.

7. If trimming with lace, fit the valance on the bed to adjust the length if necessary, then stitch the lace around the lower edge. Alternatively, turn up the hem and stitch.

8. Fit the valance on the bed, pinning the corners to hold it in place. Then take the top edge of the base piece over the head end of the bed and pin it very securely.

Take the side edges of the frill around the top corners and glue to the head end.

9. Cut a 60 × 32cm (24 × 13in) piece of corrugated card as shown on the pattern diagram for the head of the bed. To cover the card, cut a piece of satin 70cm (28in) square and join the side edges for the centre back seam. Make it into a 'bag' by matching the centre back to the centre front and then stitching across the bottom. Turn to the right side and fit the card inside, pinning temporarily to hold the base of the card in position at the bottom of the bag. Gather the top edge across the front of the bag only and draw up tightly, then pin the gathers to the top point of the card.

10. Turn the canister upside down and cut round it as indicated by the broken lines on the diagram, 3cm (1¼in) from the base, but leaving a 3cm (1¼in) wide strip the full depth of the canister. Fit the strip of wood inside this piece and tape them very securely together as shown in the second diagram.

To line the inside of the fitment neatly, cut a strip of paper 3cm (1¼in) deep and long enough to fit around the canister. Cover this with the coverlet fabric, turning a 2cm (¾in) surplus over one long edge, but leaving 5cm (2in) overlapping the other long edge. Fit this piece up inside the canister, taking the surplus smoothly over the cut edge and gluing it to the outside (cut away round the strip of wood).

Rest the fitment on top of the bed-head and tape the strip of wood very securely to the centre back of the card, then gather the remaining top edge of the satin and draw up tightly across the back.

11. Glue and pin the bed-head very securely to the top end of the bed keeping the lower edges absolutely level.

12. Beginning and ending 2cm (¾in) from the selvedge, gather across the top edge of the voile and draw up tightly. Turn to the right side. Fit over the top of the canister, to hang as illustrated, and mark the length. Draw a thread across the voile at this point to mark your cutting line, then cut.

Stitch wide lace on the right side to overlap the selvedges and lower edge, turning the corners neatly. Overlap the lace at the top and join, then catch all the gathers tightly together underneath. Turn to the right side and fit over the canister.

13. Trace a template pattern for the coronet (ignoring the broken lines). Draw it onto thin card, making it long enough to fit loosely over the draped canister. Allow an overlap as shown. Cover with coverlet fabric (see Basics 11), snipping the surplus indicated by the broken lines into V-shaped tabs and gluing them smoothly over to the back of the card. Glue the surplus fabric over the lower edge in the same way. Cover the back too, but trim the fabric level with the edge of the card.

Curve round into a circle and glue the overlap neatly. Glue pearl trimming around the lower edge, with a band of fancy braid just above; then glue more pearl trimming around the top edge (cut into short lengths and do each curve separately). Fit over the curtain and arrange the gathers.

14. For the coverlet, cut a piece of fabric 82cm (32¾in) long × the width of the bed plus 2cm (¾in). Have the length across the fabric so that you have a selvedge for one of the short edges (see cutting diagram). Fold in half as indicated by the broken line to measure 41cm (16⅜in) long, and mark the fold line (this will be the top edge).

Cut a piece of wadding 40cm (16in) long × the width of the bed. Tack this to the wrong side of one half of the fabric, level with the fold line, and with 1cm (⅜in) surplus fabric around the

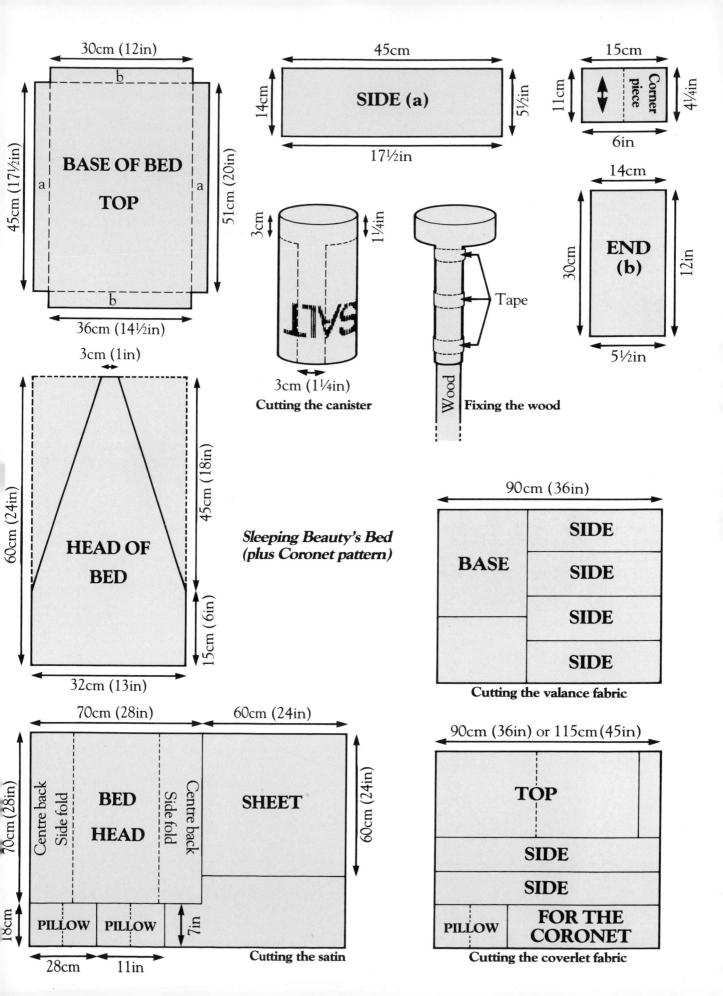

BASE OF BED
TOP

30cm (12in)

b

a

a

45cm (17½in)

51cm (20in)

b

36cm (14½in)

3cm (1in)

HEAD OF BED

60cm (24in)

45cm (18in)

15cm (6in)

32cm (13in)

45cm

SIDE (a)

14cm

5½in

17½in

3cm

1¼in

SALT

3cm (1¼in)

Cutting the canister

Tape

Wood

Fixing the wood

15cm

Corner piece

11cm

4¼in

6in

14cm

END (b)

30cm

12in

5½in

Sleeping Beauty's Bed
(plus Coronet pattern)

90cm (36in)

BASE

SIDE

SIDE

SIDE

SIDE

Cutting the valance fabric

70cm (28in)

60cm (24in)

Centre back
Side fold

BED HEAD

Centre back
Side fold

SHEET

70cm (28in)

60cm (24in)

18cm

PILLOW

PILLOW

7in

28cm

11in

Cutting the satin

90cm (36in) or 115cm (45in)

TOP

SIDE

SIDE

PILLOW

FOR THE CORONET

Cutting the coverlet fabric

edges. Fold the fabric along the fold line, right side inside, and join the sides and bottom, leaving 10cm (4in) open at the centre of the bottom edge. Trim the seams and corners, then turn to the right side. Turn the raw edges inside and slip stitch the opening.

15. Pin the top edge of the narrow lace around the sides and bottom of the coverlet, overlapping 1cm (½in) at each end, and turning the corners smoothly at a right angle. Oversew neatly together, then mark the lace equally into sixteen.

16. Cut two 14cm (5½in) deep strips across the width of the fabric for the sides (as shown on the cutting diagram). Join to form one long strip. Stitch lace along the lower edge. Mark the top edge equally into sixteen, then gather, beginning and ending 1cm (⅜in) from the side edge. Pin around the sides and bottom, behind the lace, matching the marked points. Draw up the gathers, distributing them evenly between the pins, and stitch the lower edge of the lace over the gathering line. Turn the side edges and ends of the lace under, and hem neatly.

17. Cut a 60cm (24in) square of satin for the sheet. Turn under and stitch a very narrow hem around the sides and bottom. Trim the top edge with wide lace.

18. Make two satin pillows and one to match the coverlet. For each pillow, cut a piece of fabric 18 × 28cm (7 × 11in). Keeping the right side inside, fold in half to measure 18 × 14cm (7 × 5½in). Join all around the three sides, leaving 6cm (2½in) open at the centre of one short end. Trim the seams and corners, then turn to the right side. Stuff well, but not too firmly, pushing well into the corners. Turn the raw edges inside and slip stitch the opening.

Stitch the wide lace around the edge of the single pillow, gathering generously to turn the corners. Trim the two satin pillows in the same way, using narrower lace.

19. Make two butterfly bows from 25cm (10in) lengths of ribbon (see Basics 6: mark points B 4cm (1½in) from A). Stitch to the bottom corners of the coverlet, as illustrated.

Trim the top corners of the single pillow with two more bows made from 12cm (4½in) lengths of ribbon, measuring points B 3cm (1¼in) from A. Arrange this pillow centrally on top of the two satin ones.

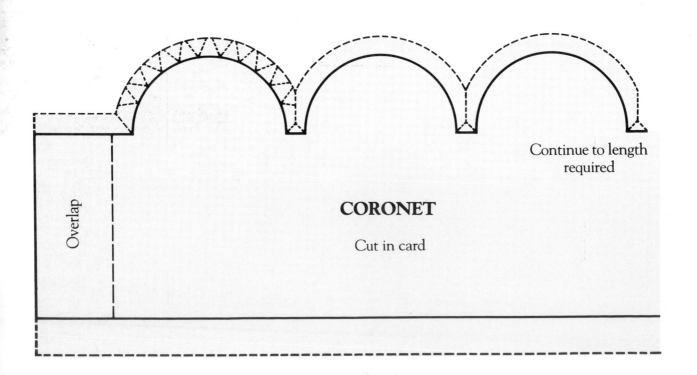

Continue to length required

CORONET

Cut in card

Overlap